WORKING GIRLS

WORKING GIRLS

•

*An Illustrated
History of
the Oldest
Profession*

NEIL PHILIP

BLOOMSBURY

For a mot who does a little typography

First published 1991 by
Bloomsbury Publishing Ltd, 2 Soho Square, London W1V 5DE

An Albion Book

Conceived, designed and produced by
The Albion Press Ltd, P.O. Box 52, Princes Risborough, Aylesbury,
Bucks HP17 9PR

Designer: Emma Bradford
Editor: Robyn Marsack
Project co-ordinator: Elizabeth Wilkes

ISBN 0-7475-1030-X

Typesetting and colour origination by York House, London
Printed and bound in Great Britain by BPCC Hazell Books, Paulton
and Aylesbury

Title page illustration:
ALFRED STEVENS: *The Bath, c. 1867*

CONTENTS

ANONYMOUS: *The Two Conditions of the World, 15th century*

PREFACE

Prostitution is as much to do with psychology as physiology. This book is an attempt to recognise that, and in doing so to provide an historical context in which the meaning and nature of prostitution in modern Western society can be explored.

I hope it will be useful in defining, for male and female readers alike, some of the issues involved, which take us to the heart of the relationship between the sexes in our society. These issues are ones of power and control, independence and servitude, money and morality, and most of them are resolvable only on an individual level. Any general statement about prostitution is likely to be both true and untrue at the same time: it empowers and degrades, liberates and enslaves, is an honest and dishonest transaction, and so on. The most one can do is let the conflicting voices make their own counterpoint.

The best and most eloquent voices are those of prostitutes themselves, and I have tried to listen most attentively to what they had to say, before looking at what historians or moralists have said about them. With admirable courage, prostitutes, from eighteenth-century women such as Ann Sheldon and Phebe Phillips through to modern campaigners such as Helen Buckingham and Dolores French, have stood up to be counted in the face of society's disapproval. The liveliness and lucidity of their accounts of their profession are a fitting rebuke to those who have argued that prostitutes suffer from some special form of "feeble-mindedness".

One of the non-prostitute sources I frequently quote is the immense sexual autobiography of the Victorian roué known only as Walter (but tentatively identified as the bibliographer Henry Spencer Ashbee). Walter's extraordinarily frank and copious confession, entitled *My Secret Life*, reveals in its rawest state the exploitation of the poor by the rich, the defenceless by the powerful, which is one of the truths of prostitution. But it is equally true that the women he frequented did very well out of him financially, and if his accounts are to be trusted, often had a good deal of fun along the way. Certainly he liked them, within the blinkered confines of his need to purchase rather than earn affection. He wrote:

> To their class I owe a debt of gratitude: they have been my refuge in sorrow, an unfailing relief in all my miseries, have saved me from drinking, gambling, and perhaps worse. I shall never throw stones at them, nor speak harshly to them, nor of them.

It has not been my intention in the chapters that follow to shock, or titillate, or lecture the reader, but simply to try to trace the human dynamics of a profession which is too often seen in terms of stereotype and melodrama. The illustrations which accompany the text, by painters such as Toulouse-Lautrec, Otto Dix, and R.B. Kitaj, and photographers such as Brassaï and Bellocq are crucial to my argument. Their images are so instinct with individual life, so sympathetic to and perceptive of their subjects, that the viewer is drawn willy-nilly into a human relationship with the girls, clients, and onlookers they portray. It is a matter for regret that no female artist has depicted brothel life with the assiduity of a Degas or a Pascin, for this is a subject which desperately needs a female perspective.

That perspective has had to be supplied in this book by the prostitutes who have written or been interviewed about their lives, and who can often tell us something we knew but had never realised about men and women. For instance, Maggie, a brothel madam in Sydney, Australia, had been a prostitute for nearly forty years when she told Roberta Perkins, "Funnily enough kissing is something the guys will pay more for, but not many of the girls will do it. They say that sexual intercourse is the closest form of communication, but it's not, it's kissing."

NEIL PHILIP
MARCH 1991

1 THE OLDEST PROFESSION

BY WAY OF INTRODUCTION

At a conference on the politics of prostitution and pornography held in Toronto in November 1985, Peggy Miller, founder of the Canadian Organisation for the Rights of Prostitutes, stood up from the floor and asked the crucial question: "What's wrong with fucking for a living?" She continued, "I like it, I can live out my fantasies . . . And I represent many other whores out there who, despite the terrible legal and social environment, enjoy our work." For many of the feminists she was addressing, such a statement must have cut to the heart of their established ideas about the prostitute as victim, and prostitution as, in the words of Susan Cole at the same conference, "an institution of male supremacy".

Margo St. James, founder of the prostitutes' pressure group COYOTE, went further: "The great fear for men, who are running things, is that if whores have a voice, suddenly good women are going to find out how much their time is worth and how to ask for the money." In fact, "I've always thought that whores were the only emancipated women."

This book reviews the history of prostitution in the modern Western world in the light of such statements. Its title, *Working Girls*, is meant to suggest its non-judgmental acceptance of prostitution as, first and foremost, a way of making a living. Writers on prostitution, depending on their perspective, may characterise prostitutes as nymphomaniacs, or mental defectives, or innocent victims. I have been interested not so much in the sorts of moral judgments which such terms imply, but in investigating the extent to which the choice of prostitution as a way of life has empowered women by offering them a chance of financial independence. Prostitution is above all else a business: women enter it through poverty, and stay in it for its financial rewards.

This angle of interest is not meant to deny the exploitation of women and children which occurs in prostitution, nor to condone the sexual climate in which prostitution thrives. Neither is it meant to supplant or rival the broader historical analyses of the recognised authorities on the subject. But it does seem worthwhile, in the light of feminist and post-feminist arguments about sexual politics and women's history, to re-examine the evidence regarding this taboo area of women's work. Because this has been my

FRANCOIS BOUCHER: *The Odalisque (Louisa O'Murphy), 1745*

intention. I have ignored male prostitution, although this offers many interesting parallels to female prostitution, and in this book unless otherwise stated the word prostitute is always intended to mean prostitute women.

Through history, of all the women who have supported themselves financially, the largest group has almost certainly been the prostitutes. It is this financial independence which as much as anything has attracted society's disapproval. Prostitution is a business which has been mostly run by women. It could be seen as a female master craft, practised in an unbroken tradition through the ages. Few other ways of making a living have changed so little over thousands of years; prostitutes today are offering exactly the same services as in the ancient world.

HENRI DE TOULOUSE-LAUTREC: *Alone, 1896*

Prostitution is hard work. Except at the most basic level, it requires skill, imagination, resourcefulness. While nineteenth-century reformers, uneasy at any expression of female sexuality, were eager to categorise prostitutes as "feeble-minded", the women attracted by such work in fact tend to be lively, intelligent and strong. Prostitutes do form an international and historical sisterhood, and feminists have surely been right to reappraise the traditional view of them as downtrodden and exploited, and recognise prostitution as a calling which, when freely entered, is as valid as any other, male-conditioned, role available to women in a patriarchal society.

Prostitutes, from the Empress Theodora on, have risen to the heights of political power; others have achieved financial or social success which would have been denied to them through any other route. And if many

E.J. Bellocq: *A woman in a Storyville brothel, c. 1912*

others have lived on and eventually sunk below the borderline of poverty and degradation, it is a moot point, as we shall see, whether their lot was any worse than that of their "good" sisters.

I hope that this book, by concentrating on the lives and feelings of prostitutes themselves, rather than on the social, moral, legal and sanitary problems which prostitution presents, will be able to reconstruct for the sensitive reader the private life as well as the public face of the prostitute over the last three centuries.

A simple anecdote from the memoirs of press photographer Percy Brown may indicate the type of material I have sought. Brown emigrated from Shrewsbury as a young man to work as a carpenter in San Francisco after the earthquake of 1906. The brothels of the Barbary Coast were among the first buildings to rise from the ruins, and Brown worked on one such, Mayor Spitz's "dollar house" at 620 Jackson Street. One day in the lunch hour he was taken back to the building by his friend John Malley, with the words, "Say, partner, let's go shopping."

A special policeman was controlling the queue of "mechanics" filing into the building's scores of cubicles. Left alone with "a pretty, dark-haired girl practically undressed", Brown handed over the desired fee but tried to make his excuses and leave. Told to "Hurry up, boy, there's a lot of business running about the floors today," he replied, "That's all right, Miss, I only came in to have a look round with my friend John. We built this place."

The girl, her professional pride dented, became abusive, and the embarrassed Percy had to be rescued by his friend. In a saloon afterwards, however, John picked a quarrel with him, shouting. "You son of bitch, you think you're the worm's hips, packing dollars in a sock to beat it back home." A vicious fight ensued.

Later, Brown asked his friend why he had lost his temper:

> "Because you didn't pay the kid," he replied shortly.
> "But I gave her three dollars, all she asked me for," I replied.
> He stared hard at me and said, "Well shake me for the biggest darn fool, I took you for one of those emigrant cheap skates who waste the girls' time and don't pass them a cent. Partner, believe me, I'm sorry. Shake."

This little story is scarcely a typical account of a meeting between prostitute and client. But its crosscurrents allow us for a moment to see all the characters – Percy, the girl, John, even the policeman and the silent "mechanics" – in human terms. The literature of prostitution, whether moralistic, confessional or titillatory, can seem not just lubricious and prying but entirely removed from everyday experience. Yet as Percy Brown shows, the actors in each encounter *are* real people with feelings and tempers and senses of humour. For John, the girl in Mayor Spitz's house was a fellow worker, entitled to decent, honest treatment. It is as "working girls" that prostitutes see themselves, and it is as workers that this book will consider them. It will concentrate not on voyeuristic sexual description, but on the turn of phrase or telling detail which enables us to see the human beings behind the commercial transaction, with the clarity with which we recognise in Toulouse-Lautrec's drawings of his prostitute friends, living women rather than anonymous whores.

The origins of prostitution are lost in antiquity. The earliest references are to ritual prostitution in the service of fertility deities, such as that described in Babylon by Herodotus in the fifth century BC:

> There is one custom amongst these people which is wholly shameful: every woman who is a native of the country must once in her life go and sit in the temple of Aphrodite and there give herself to a strange man . . . Once a woman has taken her seat she is not allowed to go home until a man has thrown a silver coin into her lap and taken her outside to lie with him.

Such temple prostitution probably co-existed in early societies with commercial prostitution, and has little to do with the development of prostitution in Western society, the main attributes of which we find clearly established in Ancient Greece and Rome. The surviving brothel at Pompeii, with its wall paintings depicting the various services available within, was clearly not much different from its counterparts today. Athenaeus's account of an Athenian brothel in the fourth century BC has a totally familiar ring:

> Any man can pick out the one that pleases him – thin, fat, plump, lanky, crooked, young, old, middle-sized, ripe . . . They drag you into the house willy-nilly, calling you "daddy" if you are an old man or "little brother" or "little lad". And you can have any of them for a small sum, without any risk.

The serried ranks of Roman whores included those streetwalkers who catered to their clients in the *fornices*, the arches in the walls of public buildings, thus giving us the term fornicate for sexual intercourse. The writings of Ovid, Petronius, Suetonius and Juvenal give a vivid picture of the sexual life of their time, and of the extent to which prostitution permeated the ancient world: Messalina, wife of the Emperor Claudius, for instance,

WALL-PAINTING: *Lovers, Pompeii, 1st century* AD

regularly took her place, for kicks, in Rome's lowest brothels, once challenging the most experienced prostitutes in the city to a contest to see who could cater to the greatest number of men in a single session; Messalina won.

The basic structure of ancient prostitution, with its streetwalkers, brothels ranging from the functional to the luxurious, and high-class courtesans, remains recognisable today. So, too, do the problems which attended it: the threat to public order and propriety, and the danger to health from venereal disease. But though there was regulation of prostitution, there was no thought of eradicating it.

In the later Roman Empire, a prostitute even rose to the pinnacle of power. The Empress Theodora, one of the most fascinating figures of her era, started life as a child prostitute at the Hippodrome in Byzantium, where her father was a bear-keeper. According to Procopius:

> Now for a time Theodora was still too immature to sleep with a man or to have intercourse like a woman, but she acted as might a male prostitute to satisfy those dregs of humanity, slaves though they were, who followed their master to the theatre and there took the opportunity to indulge in such bestial practices, and she remained some considerable time in a brothel, given over to such unnatural traffic of the body . . . But as soon as she reached maturity she joined the women of the stage and became a harlot, of the kind that our ancestors used to call "the infantry".

Theodora's finest moment came when she ruthlessly put down the Nika revolt in AD 532, when her husband Justinian was ready to flee. Her speech rejecting flight gives a good idea of her strength of character, which had that compelling quality which we now call charisma:

> Every man who is born into the light of day must sooner or later die: and how could an Emperor ever allow himself to be a fugitive? May I myself never willingly shed my imperial robes, nor see the day when I am no longer addressed by my title. If you, my Lord, wish to save your skin, you will have no difficulty in doing so. We are rich, there is the sea, there too are our ships. But consider first whether, when you reach safety, you will not regret that you did not choose death in preference. As for me, I stand by the ancient saying: the purple is the noblest winding-sheet.

Interestingly, one of Theodora's acts as Empress was to order five hundred of Byzantium's prostitutes to enter a convent known as "The Repentance" on the far shore of the Bosporus, a fate which drove some of them, possibly through boredom, "to cut short their chances of redemption by jumping at night into the sea."

Theodora's cold treatment of her erstwhile colleagues reflects the strength of Christianity's antipathy to sexuality. While St Augustine was ready to accept prostitution on the grounds that if it were suppressed, "capricious lusts will overthrow society", the free and easy sexual world of the Greeks and Romans was challenged by Christianity's new ethic of guilt and shame. Recognising this, the Prefect Hierocles in Egypt used to sentence early Christian women to compulsory prostitution. Conversely, numbers of prostitutes converted to the new religion, among them many of the church's early saints, such as St Mary of Egypt, St Palagia, St Theodatea, St Afra and St Mary the Harlot.

Christianity's disapproval of the very fact that we are sexual beings was one ingredient necessary to turn the open and practical prostitution of the ancient world (with all its manifest injustices such as the sexual exploitation of slaves) into the furtive, hangdog trade of the modern Western world. The other was the development of industrial capitalism, in which women's sexuality became simply one more asset for the owning classes to exploit and the proletariat to sell. This book will trace both these forces at work, while acknowledging the way in which many prostitutes managed to use male guilt, greed and desire not simply just to turn an honest penny but also to assert and extend their own independence and individuality.

In some ways we have more information about the lives of prostitutes in the past than we do about most other types of women. Prostitution has always been a subject of illicit interest, and it has always, too, been illegal and therefore the activities and words of prostitutes survive in official records. But the voice of the prostitute herself is often muffled and distorted. While some high-class courtesans – such as Cora Pearl and Harriette Wilson – left memoirs, most of the countless working girls of the past centuries have vanished into the great silence.

For that reason alone it behoves us to listen to someone like Nell, when she tells Priscilla Alexander:

> I know my value, you see, I know my worth. When you're making money for yourself, there's an immediate value on you, you're selling yourself, your personality, your charms, your appearance, your ability to persuade, your ability to sell. It takes skill, definite skill, and a lot of strength. I've come to appreciate those qualities in myself.

2 GAY LADIES AND DOLLYMOPS

PROSTITUTION IN BRITAIN

The modern history of prostitution in Britain starts, perhaps, with the "Ordinance for the Government of the Stews in the Bishop of Winchester's Liberty of the Clink on the Bankside in Southwark" issued in 1161 by Henry II's parliament, and endorsed by the Archbishop of Canterbury and Thomas à Becket. There were sixty-four ordinances, designed to encourage a civilised and well-regulated trade. Stewholders, as brothel-keepers were known, were forbidden to charge more than fourteen pence a week for a room, or to employ married women or nuns. Prostitutes were expected to live elsewhere, and to treat the brothel as a place of work. Several of the rules were explicitly aimed at preventing any woman's being pressed into or kept in prostitution against her will. Perhaps the most interesting of all was the requirement that each transaction should be for the whole night.

The Southwark stews, as their name suggests, occupied the site of the old Roman baths, which had doubled as bordellos. By 1161 they had already operated "from time out of mind", and Southwark remained one of the chief areas of London prostitution until the sixteenth century. Throughout this period, the brothels operated on land owned by the Bishop of Winchester. Cock Lane in Smithfield was the other legally recognised prostitution district, but contemporary records show that prostitution was by no means restricted to the approved areas, as straightforward City street names such as Gropecuntlane attest.

The spread and development of prostitution in London has been well documented in E.J. Burford, *London: The Synfulle Citie*. Despite various half-hearted attempts to regulate or stamp out the trade, small brothels thrived, and streetwalkers openly solicited at public entertainments, including executions. A broadsheet of 1661 describes "Bonny Bess of Whore and Bacon Lane . . . and Merry Moll of Ducke Street . . . who sat at the wayside with their Leggs spreade wide crying 'Here's your Ware, Boys!'"

By the Restoration of Charles II in 1661, the general climate of licentiousness can be gauged by the open publication of a guide to London's brothels and prostitutes, John Garfield's *The Wand'ring Whore*, based on Aretino's *Puttana Errante*.

The rakes who gathered in such taverns as Lockett's and the Bear would,

STUDIO OF SIR PETER LELY: *Nell Gwyn, c. 1670*

according to Henry Bulkely, later Master of the King's Household, "talk of nothing but fighting and fucking", and their attitude to life has been perfectly expressed by the epitome of their class, John Wilmot, Earl of Rochester:

> Cupid and Bacchus my saints are:
> May drink and love still reign.
> With wine I wash away my cares.
> And then to cunt again.

The most famous of all the whores of her day was Nell Gwyn, an actress who began her career in Mother Ross's brothel and ended it as the king's mistress. According to Bishop Burnet, Nell,

> the indiscreetest and wildest creature that ever was in court, continued to the end of the king's life in great favour, and was maintained at a vast expense. The duke of Buckingham told me, that when she was first brought to the king, she asked only five hundred pounds a year: and the king refused it. But when he told me this, about four years after, he said, she had got of the king above sixty thousand pounds. She acted all persons in so lively a manner, and was such a constant diversion to the king, that even a new mistress could not drive her away. But after all he never treated her with the decencies of a mistress, but rather with the lewdness of a prostitute: as she had been indeed to a great many: and therefore she called the king her Charles the third. Since she had formerly been kept by two of that name.

Nell's bedroom in St James's Square was mirrored on both the walls and the ceiling, useful aids in stimulating the avid but jaded desires of her monarch. Rochester records, in his scabrous "Satyr on Charles II",

> The pains it costs to poor, laborious Nelly,
> Whilst she employs hands, fingers, mouth, and thighs,
> Ere she can raise the member she enjoys.

Her reward, at least in popular belief, was the king's deathbed instruction, "Let not poor Nelly starve."

Nell Gwyn, although she came from a poor background, is typical of the high-class prostitutes who played such a significant role in English social life over the next two centuries. These women used their wit and accomplishments, as much as their physical charms, to dominate the lives of England's aristocracy, and many of them married into it; even Nell Gwyn was the mother of two dukes. In essence they acted as paid mistresses to a succession of nobles rather than as common prostitutes. Though the distinction blurs in many cases, it was recognised in the phrase of a writer in 1607, who explained that, "Your whore is for every rascal, but your courtesan is for your courtier."

Inevitably, more is known of individual courtesans than of whores, and more of those who operated in London than those elsewhere. However, G.R. Quaife's detailed study of Somerset court records from 1601 to 1660 does give us a very interesting picture of prostitution in the seventeenth-century countryside. He distinguishes four kinds of rural prostitute: the vagrant whore, the public whore (who worked from an inn), the private whore and the village whore. An example of the village whore is Isobel Watt of Tolland, who said, "she would open her door at any time of the night either to a married man or young man". In contrast to such neighbourly behaviour was the more aggressive sales technique of the vagrant whore, such as Lucy Francis, who visited weavers in their homes or shops. She entered one such establishment and, "putting her back towards the side of the looms said these words: viz. Here is a good place to go at trading. This examinant asking her why, she answered, because there was good footing for that she could not slide."

This *ad hoc* freelance prostitution remained the pattern in the English countryside for the next two centuries. Village whores were often widows, tolerated by the local community as a sexual safety valve. But it was in towns and cities that prostitution most thrived, attracting many country girls to the chief population centres. By the eighteenth century, when London's centre of prostitution had moved to Covent Garden, we have entered the world of Hogarth and Fanny Hill, where, according to a contemporary ballad, "At every corner of the street there's Whores eight o'Penny."

Regular lists of prostitutes were distributed yearly to a wide clientele. One such, *Ranger's Impartial List of the Ladies of Pleasure of Edinburgh*, published in 1775 and attributed to James Tytler, yields a good deal of information about the organisation and extent of prostitution at the time. One interesting feature is that all the brothel-keepers are women: Mrs Japp, Miss Adams, Miss Walker, Miss Forsyth, Mrs Tenant, Miss Tibby Nairn, Mrs Tait, Mrs Young and Miss Witherspoon ran the nine main houses. Tibby Nairn's brothel in Fowles's Close was regarded as "the genteelest" of them all. Its eight girls included several very young ones, such as sixteen-year-old Miss Fraser, "as pretty a little filly as man ever clapped leg over".

Miss Walker, who kept a brothel in Bess Wynd, is termed "disobliging",

WILLIAM HOGARTH: *The Four Times of Day – Morning, 1738*

while her girls are rated as follows; Miss Peggy Bruce: "not a bad penny-worth for any gentleman"; Miss Betsy Clark: "sulky temper"; Miss Blair: "understands her business very well"; Miss Stephenson: "very eager in the Critical Minute"; Miss Gilmor: "for the most part, gives satisfaction"; Miss Galloway: "thick and short"; Miss Sutherland: "an old veteran" (she was thirty); Miss Inglis: "she is remarkably fond of performing on the silent flute, and can manage the stops extraordinarily well. She twists you round like an eel, and would not loose a drop of the precious juice of nature, not for a kingdom".

The writer pulls even fewer punches in his description of Mrs *alias* Lady, Agnew of Nether-bow, one of Edinburgh's independent prostitutes. The viciousness of his attack on her is interesting for several reasons, most notably in the fact that his contempt is chiefly stirred by her unashamed sexuality. The ideal prostitute, to this customer's eyes, was not a sexual being in her own right, but rather a conduit for the sexuality of her client. He writes:

> This drunken bundle of iniquity, is about 50 years of age, lusty and tall, and she has followed the old trade since she was about 13. One thing she can boast of, that she is the daughter of a late worthy Baronet, who was a brave General in the war before last. Being a disgrace to her relations, who are some of the best in Scotland, they sent her to the north, where she continued her business for a long time. She regards neither decency nor decorum, and would as willingly lie with a chimney-sweep as with a Lord. Her desires are so immoderate, that she would think nothing of a company of Grenadiers at one time. Take her all in all, she is an abandoned Piece.

Behind the animus of this account, an intriguing life can be glimpsed. Mrs Agnew appears to have rebelled completely against the expectations of her background, to have taken to prostitution from her own inclination and choice, and to have remained a prostitute for about forty years.

A foreign visitor, J. W. v. Archenholtz, gives a grim picture of street prostitution in London in the late eighteenth century, including the fate of the poor "dress-lodgers" who did not even own their own clothes, and who were deliberately kept in debt to the house. He writes:

> So soon as it becomes dark, these girls, well turned-out, in all seasons flood the principal streets and squares of the town. Many go on the man-hunt in borrowed clothes which they hire by the day from the matrons, who for safety's sake pay another woman to follow the huntress continuously on

foot in order to see that she does not run away with the clothes. If the girl makes no capture and comes home without money, she will be ill-treated and must go hungry. They therefore accost passers-by and take them either home or to the taverns. They can be seen standing in groups. The best class of prostitutes, who live independently, are content to go on their way till they are spoken to. Many married women even, who live in distant parts of the town, come to the Westminster district where they are unknown, and carry on the profession, either from vice or need. I have been astounded to see children of eight and nine years offer their company, at least so far as it would serve. The corruption of men's hearts is so great, that even such children can find lovers to flirt with them. More than that: at midnight the girls leave the streets and old beggar women of 60 and more come out from their hiding places in order to serve drunken men returning heated from their revels, who must satisfy their animal needs blindly, as it were, "at a galop".

A broadside ballad, "The Poor Whores Lament", puts their case with haunting authenticity:

> Come listen a while and you shall hear,
>   How the poor Whores fare in the winter
> They've hardly got any rags to hide their ware
>   Indeed tis a despret thing Sir.
> With their draggel tales thats nine inches deep,
>   And hardly a shooe or a stocking,
> Yet if a Cull they by chance should meet,
>   At him they will be bobing.

It may be thought that the scene in the brothels was more sophisticated than this, but the main difference seems to have been in the furnishings. Phebe Phillips, a prostitute whose 1809 memoirs *The Woman of the Town*, written under the pseudonym Maria Maitland, offer one of the sparkiest first-hand accounts of English prostitution, describes the typical turn-of-the-century brothel as a place which, while it offered lively diversion to the young blades of the town, was a dreary grind for the girls who worked there:

> The boarders of these houses are obliged to sit up every morning (unless particularly employed) until four or five o'clock, for the good of the house, to drink with any straggling buck, that may reel in at any of the early morning hours. With them they are obliged to sit down, drink, and bear

whatever behaviour these drunken visitants are pleased to use: and at last, if they be in luck, put to bed some fellow who has swallowed too many bumpers to suffer himself to be sensible of the wretchedness he must inevitably endure from a most impure connection.

One if left as so often with the feeling that the chief disparity between the prostitutes and their clients was that the girls were much more intelligent and thoughtful than the men. Certainly, Phebe Phillip's contemporary Harriette Wilson, whose own *Memoirs* have the status of a minor classic, was a most remarkably vivacious and attractive personality, whose account of her life lacks the edge of bitterness which Phebe's more incisive mind brought to her experience. For a time after the Battle of Trafalgar, Harriette, her sister Fanny, and their friend Julia Storer, known as Julia Johnstone, were hailed as "the Three Graces" of fashionable London. The Duke of Wellington approached the brothel-keeper Mrs Porter of Berkeley Square and begged her, as "one of her oldest customers", to arrange for him to meet Harriette; she, less impressed by him than he by her, likened him to "a rat-catcher". Harriette paints a good picture of Julia:

> She was certainly one of the best mannered women in England, not excepting those of the very highest rank. She had the most delicately fair skin, and the prettiest arms, hands, and feet, and the most graceful form, which could well be imagined; but her features were not regular, nor their expression particularly good. She struck me as a woman of very violent passions, combined with an extremely shy and reserved disposition.

Julia published her own *Confessions* in 1825.

Harriette was one of fifteen children of a poor Swiss clockmaker in Mayfair. Her sisters Amy, Fanny and Sophia were also prostitutes, specialising in extorting as much money as possible from rich and powerful men for the least return in physical services. Amy Wilson's arrangement with Count Palmella, the Portuguese ambassador, was typical. Her terms, robustly stated, were "two hundred pounds a month, paid in advance, and the use of his horses and carriage". Also typical was the fact that Amy took the first two hundred pounds but failed to deliver her side of the bargain.

It may be argued that such courtesans scarcely lived in the same world as the streetwalkers who teemed in London's streets, but in fact the worlds, as Wellington's approach to Mrs Porter indicates, did intermesh, and Harriette recognised this. At her own lowest ebb, she took in a streetwalker who lived "by the prostitution of her person to unfeeling and drunken strangers", regarding her straightforwardly as "a sister in affliction". Ann Sheldon's slightly earlier memoirs recount how she kept a sort of private brothel for Lord Grosvenor in Lambeth, who would send her orders to round up girls to satisfy whatever fancy happened to take him. For instance: "He sent a desire that I would collect a group of pea-pickers for his choice, and my garrets were instantly furnished with a tribe of them for the noble Lord's inspection." It will be noted that it was assumed – as it later is in the memoirs of the late Victorian roué Walter – that any working-class woman or girl will be sexually available to a rich man. As William Cobbett wrote, nine-tenths of all English boys and girls, "must live by manual labour, or become thieves and strumpets".

By the mid-nineteenth century, prostitution was endemic to English society. The low wages, long hours and horrendous working conditions in most occupations open to working-class women meant that prostitution was necessary for many simply to make ends meet. For instance, the great social investigator Henry Mayhew interviewed a woman who earned three shillings a week making cotton moleskin and cord trousers:

> I do the best I can with what little money I earn, and the rest I am obligated to go to the streets for. That is true, though I says it as shouldn't. I can't get a rag to wear without flying to prostitution for it. My wages will barely find me in food.

Such women were easy prey for wealthy men such as Walter, on the look out for "cheap quim".

One of the things which emerges clearly from Walter's accounts is the economic pressures towards prostitution in a society in which women had few other means of earning a living wage. Some occupations, such as street-vending of fruit, were little more than covers for prostitution. The flower-girls and watercress-sellers whom we admire in Victorian paintings and engravings could scarcely have made a living in their avowed profession; watercress was popular because it was the cheapest stock you could buy. Lace-makers, too, used their ability to sit in doorways apparently respectably at work to ply another trade, as the teenage Walter and his cousin Fred found out:

> One day we rode to the market-town, and, putting up our horses, strolled about. Fred said, "Let's both go and have a shove." "Where are the girls?" said I. "Oh! I know, lend me some money." "I only have ten shillings." "That is more than we shall want." We went down a lane past the Town-Hall, by

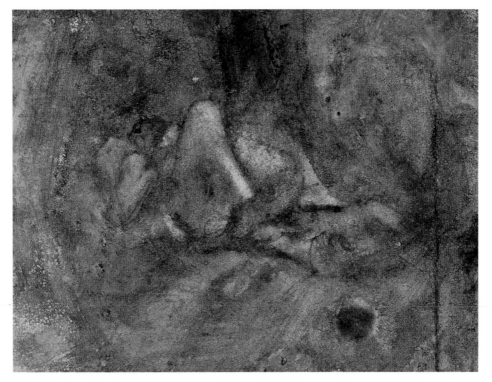

J.M.W. TURNER: *Colour sketch (lovers on a bed), c. 1830*

white-washed little cottages, at which girls were sitting or standing at the
doors making a sort of lace. "Do you see the girl you like?" said he. "Why,
they are lacemakers." "Yes, but some of them fuck for all that; there is the
one I had with the last half a-crown you lent me." Two girls were standing,
together; they nodded. "Let's try them," said Fred. We went into the cottage;
it was a new experience to me.

It was the poorest and hardest-worked Victorian girls – from field and
factory workers to domestic slaveys, dressmakers and milliners – who were
most cruelly tempted by the easier money to be earned on the streets; to
turn "gay", in the parlance of the day.

In 1862, Henry Mayhew estimated that there were over 80,000 women
working as prostitutes in London, supplemented by an inestimable number
of part-timers known as "dollymops". Some areas of London, such as Regent
Street (which was known as "the stretch") and the Haymarket, were
crammed with "gay" women who would openly accost male passers-by, as
the diaries of the barrister-poet A.J. Munby record, offering fellatio among
other services.

In 1857, the journalist and novelist Albert Smith wrote in Dickens's *Household Words* that the Haymarket "is always an offensive place to pass, even in the daytime; but at night it is absolutely hideous, with its sparring snobs, and flashing satins, and sporting gents, and painted cheeks, and brandy-sparkling eyes, and bad tobacco, and hoarse horse-laughs, and loud indecency." One may doubt whether Smith, a cheerful vulgarian, found the scene quite so offensive as all that; the tone of moral disapproval was required.

The fourth volume of Mayhew's *London Labour and the London Poor* contains many interviews with Haymarket prostitutes conducted by the novelist Bracebridge Hemyng. One, known as "Swindling Sal", told him her story:

> I was a servant gal away down in Birmingham. I got tired of workin' and slavin' to make a livin', and getting a_____ bad one at that; what o' five pun' a year and yer grub, I'd sooner starve, I would. After a bit I went to Coventry, cut Brummagem, as we calls it in those parts, and took up with the soldiers as was quartered there. I soon got tired of them. Soldiers is good – soldiers is – to walk with and that, but they don't pay; cos why, they ain't got no

WILLIAM M'CONNELL: *Two o'clock p.m., Regent Street, 1859*

money; so I says to myself, I'll go to Lunnon, and I did. I soon found my level there.

Her friend "Lushing Loo" was less forthcoming when asked for her story: "'Oh, I'm a seduced milliner,' she said, rather impatiently; 'anything you like.'"

Not all prostitutes were full-time. Walter had a long liaison with Sarah, a married actress whom he picked up in Regent Street; she worked as an artist's model for Etty and Frost. Many servant-maids, nurse-maids, shop girls and milliners supplemented their income with casual prostitution, and Hemyng interviewed one such "dollymop" who worked as a typesetter in Fleet Street on "a celebrated London morning journal". She told him that she got "enough money to live on comfortably", and she seems to have taken to occasional streetwalking from a sense of fun as much as from need. She said:

> I sometimes go to the Haymarket, either early in the evening, or early in the morning, when I can get away from the printing; and sometimes I do a little in the daytime. This is not a frequent practice of mine; I only do it when I want money to buy anything . . . I've hooked many a man by showing my ankle on a wet day.

She was nineteen, and engaged to be married to a colleague who knew nothing of her Haymarket ventures, but she told Hemyng that, "I shan't think anything of all this when I'm married." Her cheerful self-portrait was that, "I'm only a mot who does a little typography by way of variety."

Because so much Victorian prostitution arises out of the abject misery of the poor, it is important to see that the prostitution may well have tended to alleviate rather than increase that misery. One woman, aged over forty, who had been gay since she was sixteen, told Bracebridge Hemyng exactly why she clung to the life:

> I don't leave off this sort of life because I'm in a manner used to it, and what could I do if I did? I've no character [reference]; I've never been used to do anything, and I don't see what employment I stand a chance of getting. Then if I had to sit hours and hours all day long, and part of the night too, sewing or anything like that, I should get tired. It would worrit me so; never having been accustomed, you see. I couldn't stand it.

To grow old in the trade though, was not to be recommended, and most women aimed to marry and retire, or open some small business, by their thirties. There were indeed, as another of Mayhew's contributors, John Binny, noted, brothels which specialised in old women, "withered crones" who "indulge in the grossest indecencies", but these were sordid places. Older prostitutes found themselves reduced to plying for hire in London's public parks, where they must "submit to any species of humiliation for the sake of acquiring a few shillings".

Outside of London, the clearest picture we have of Victorian prostitution is in York, where Frances Finnegan has made a close and discerning study of surviving records to build up a picture of prostitution in the provincial city between 1837 and 1887. She has identified from local records 1,400 individual prostitutes and brothelkeepers in York for this period (during which York's population nearly doubled from just over 25,000 to nearly 50,000). Sixty per cent of these prostitutes were under twenty years of age, and relatively few were still active in prostitution beyond the age of thirty. Fifty per cent of the girls came from elsewhere, and forty per cent of their recorded clients were visitors to the city.

Because her evidence is mainly from court records and newspaper reports, Frances Finnegan's study catches prostitutes in moments of distress, being arrested for drunkenness or tried for theft from customers (they often worked in pairs to "roll" drunken clients), and this may influence her strongly-held view that the future held little for them but "drink, destitution and disease". While her account of their lives brilliantly shows the degradation of the impoverished poor in Victorian society, it does not to my mind prove that prostitutes were worse off than their more manageable sisters. There is something admirable in the cussed independence of a reprobate like Ann Sharpe, who, sentenced to seven years transportation on a theft charge in 1852, rewarded the judge with the words, "Thank thee, thou old bugger. I hope thou'll sit there till I come back and I'll bring thee a long tailed monkey to play with." Victorian sources emphasise the wretched and vicious state of the criminal poor – "thieves, prostitutes and cadgers" – but episodes such as this also ring with a stubborn wit and resilience.

At the other end of the social scale, London offered high-class brothels such as Kate Hamilton's, together with a handful of *grandes horizontales* who recalled the courtesans of a century before. One English girl, Cora Pearl, born Emma Crouch, had the whole of Paris at her feet. The exploits of such women were the common gossip of the day, as Thomas Hardy remembered from his early months in London in 1862:

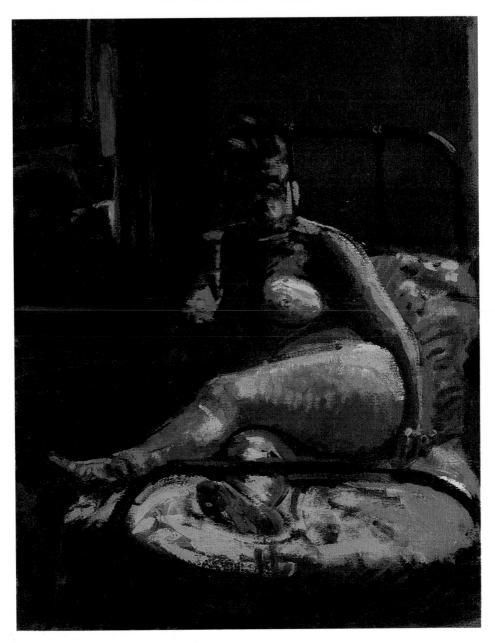

WALTER SICKERT: *La Hollandaise, c. 1906*

The ladies talked about by the architects' pupils and other young men into whose society Hardy was thrown were Cora Pearl, "Skittles", Agnes Willoughby, Adah Isaacs Menken, and others successively, of whom they professed to know many romantic and *risqué* details but really knew nothing at all.

Skittles, whose real name was Catherine Walters, was born of humble parents in Liverpool in 1839, but such was her poise and character that her conquests were to include the Prince of Wales. Walter, too, patronised Skittles, and tells us that she "took a fancy to me, but her foul tongue shocked me". Altogether, Walter's considered view was that "There is wonderfully little difference between the woman you have for five shillings, and the one you pay five pounds, excepting in the silk, linen, and manners." Five shillings was still, of course, a considerable sum, equivalent to half a week's wages for an agricultural labourer.

The First World War, the great fracture of modern history, brought change to the prostitution scene as to the rest of society. The Victorian repressions which found their guilty expression in the vast underworld of illicit sexuality were eroded, while women in turn occupied a new position in society. The increased value placed on women's work in munitions factories and elsewhere sounded the death knell for the semi-slavery of domestic service, which had been so intricately bound up with the creation and supply of Victorian prostitutes. In addition, a new sexual freedom had dawned, and soldiers returning from the front found their sweethearts ready to sleep with them, and offering something more meaningful than the hasty mass copulation available in military brothels.

The double standard, of course, remained. While men were expected to "sow their wild oats", there was intense social and family pressure on girls to remain chaste. Public disapproval of sexual licence was embodied in the work of purity campaigners between the wars, who whipped up public feeling by playing on fears of the White Slave Trade. Nevertheless, the 1920s, age of flappers and ragtime, saw a general loosening of sexual morals, and while of course street prostitution continued, the virtual prostitution of an entire class, which characterised the Victorian era, had disappeared.

More typical of the 1920s was a nightclub such as the 43, opened after the First World War in Gerrard Street by Kate Meyrick. Her "dance hostesses" – most of whom she claimed were "straight" – were recruited from the middle classes:

> Blondes, brunettes and red-heads, slim and Junoesque; calm of temperament and mercurial – I had to have girls to suit all sorts of men in all sorts of moods. Moreover it was necessary that they possess charm as well as mere

good looks, and I liked them to have some culture in addition. Many of the girls who worked in my clubs gained no small fame either for looks or for wit, and often for both.

A good picture of the post-war streetwalker can be found in Sheila Cousins's 1938 autobiography, *To Beg I am Ashamed*. Born in 1910 into a "good family" (though her mother, a clergyman's daughter, had also, it turned out, worked as a prostitute), Sheila Cousins regarded streetwalking as "a job like any other, a way of keeping alive. It is neither much more nor much less secure than most women's jobs." The ordinary man, who had provided the bulk of trade for the Victorian streetwalker, had been replaced by "the rejects, the neurotics, the cast-outs", from whom, "without much effort", Sheila Cousins could make a comfortable income of £10 a week. The major drawback to the job, from her point of view, was neither the working conditions nor the sex, but having to endure from her customers, "the same unending gramophone record of male plaintiveness and pity and boastfulness and desire".

Female emancipation, and the entry of women into many new fields of employment, created a new context for prostitution in which it was not the only choice facing a poor girl, but simply one among many. It started, as one can see both with Sheila Cousins and Mrs Meyrick's hostesses, a trend which has continued to the present day, of girls with good education and background turning to prostitution out of preference rather than destitution. The massage businesses which boomed in the 1960s, 1970s and 1980s were staffed by lively students, housewives and secretaries, not the frozen, starved and stupefied bundles of rags who haunted Victoria's parks. Escort agencies recruited among students, nurses and au pair girls, and offered, as one escort, Vanessa, told Jeremy Sandford, "a means of giving you social mobility". Helen Buckingham, a call-girl who has played a major role in prostitutes' pressure groups, told Sandford:

> A lot of the normal prostitutes are drawn from the working-classes and the lower middle-classes, but they've transcended their background and have an enormous amount of personality and style . . . The average prostitute reads. A lot of them read a great deal. They're interested in politics, literature and things like that. Most of them are very perky and full of life and great conversationalists.

Girls working as hostesses in London clubs, for instance, had to be lively, intelligent and attractive. In most such establishments, the girls were organised in a parody of the public school ethos, with the head hostess referred to as the Head Girl, or the Headmistress.

One new element on the London scene in the 1970s and 1980s was the presence of oil-rich Arabs, who provided a completely new free-spending clientele, and many girls concentrated on this business, despite the clients' frequently reported preference for anal intercourse. Other new markets opened up, such as the conference scene, and some girls specialised in working this circuit. One, Stella Anderson, told Sandford that the method was to book a room on the same floor as the conference delegates and then simply ring round the rooms. She reckoned that she could see five men in the evening and two more in the morning at £10 a time, deducting £5 for the room and backhanders for the porter and waiter. This sort of specialised work requires a good deal of business organisation and an alert mind; as Stella said, "You need brains to be a conference girl."

In the meantime, more traditional forms of prostitution remained. Though most of the Soho streetwalkers had been driven indoors by the 1959 Street Offences Act, gradually new patches of street activity emerged. Currently the chief areas for street prostitution in London are King's Cross and the Edgware Road, but in the 1970s the key area was Shepherd Market, where Gloria Lovatt worked. In her book *A Nice Girl Like Me* she describes how, "Men went to the Market looking for prostitutes and if you stood around for ten minutes you could guarantee someone would come up to you and ask you, 'How much?' " In less obvious areas of street prostitution, such as London's street markets, men might test the water more obliquely, with a question such as, "Are you working?"

Gloria Lovatt – who has since married and settled down – describes one very interesting local prostitution tradition in her home town of Liverpool, the time-honoured custom of "ship-visiting", a semi-prostitution in which local girls take temporary "boyfriends" while ships are in port. Usually there are enough girls to cater for all the sailors, but when not, the system reverts to a more conventional prostitution; Gloria records one instance in which she served sixty sailors on one Chinese ship in four hours, at £5 a time.

Such a low price as £5 may seem surprising when press reports so often focus on "£1000 a night" call-girls such as the House of Commons researcher Pamella Bordes, today's equivalent of the grand courtesans of the past, but while street prostitutes can make very good money compared to any regular job they could get, their charges are low. One of the many ways in which prostitution resembles the catering trade is that clients may

PAUL GOPAL-CHOWDHURY: *The Proposition, Shoreditch, 1989-90*

choose between an expensive, exclusive product or a cheap, high-turnover one. The end result is the same – the customer is fed, the client satisfied – but the atmosphere, surroundings and quality of experience are quite different.

One of the best studies of contemporary prostitution in Britain was carried out by Eileen McLeod in Birmingham in the early 1980s. The standard charge in a car was £5, while indoors, a Sheffield prostitute called Mary told her, "It's £10 for straight sex, £15 for strip and sex. If they want owt kinky the price is extra £10 or £5, it depends how much you can get out of them." A woman working outdoors could earn £100-150 a week, and indoors £200-250. As Eileen McLeod writes, "Setting these figures against the up to date figures for average earnings shows that prostitutes' earnings place them in the middle to high income band compared with men's earnings."

One girl, Julie, gave her a typical account of a modern English girl's entry into prostitution:

> I went into this because I wanted a lot of things – a car, a house and to travel, and the only way I could see to get the money fairly quickly was to do this, not having much education or being particularly skilled. I was working as a barmaid for £3 a night when I was 18 (now aged 25). I knew a girl who came into the club and she dressed very well, and I asked her what she did. She said, "I work in a sauna and I earn £100 a week." I thought, "Rubbish: no one earns £100 a week. Even the Prime Minister doesn't earn £100 a week." "Yes," she said, "I do." I never thought any more of it until one day I saw an advertisement in the Birmingham Mail which said, "Attractive, well spoken, pleasant ladies required to train as masseuses." I thought, "That could be me" so I 'phoned up, went for an interview, got the job and stayed.

The very ordinariness of the women interviewed by Eileen McLeod tells its own story about contemporary prostitution in Britain. Many of those working as prostitutes are either supplementing low incomes as students or nurses, or are single parents who can organise their working day around housework and childcare. The advantages are summarised by Carol:

> You're your own boss. You choose yourself when you want to work. When you do, you do. If you don't, you don't. If you've got a lot of commitments and a load of bills you can go out to work. If you don't want to you don't have to, you've got nobody saying you've got to clock in, you've got to clock out, which if you've got children or family commitments is quite nice.

3 JELLY ROLL BLUES

PROSTITUTION IN THE UNITED STATES

The puritan settlement of North America did not keep illicit sex at bay for long. Soon, Cotton Mather was noting in his diary that "There has been this last Week, a remarkable Instance of the divine Judgments on an infamous Harlott. There are more of her Tribe, and their bewitched Followers, in the neighbourhood." In 1753, Hannah Dilley of Boston, aged sixty, was convicted of using her home "for Letchery Fornication" and procuring whores. Benjamin Franklin was to worry in later life that he had compromised his health by "intrigues with low women" in his youth.

Nevertheless, prostitution remained a containable, local problem for some time. Outside the seaport towns such as Boston – where the Hill was known in the eighteenth century as "Mount Whoredom" – and a few cities such as New York, where prostitution inevitably surfaced, strong social disapproval kept vice at bay. The *Secret Diary* of William Byrd of Virginia, a very strongly-sexed man, shows that in 1720 he failed completely in his attempt to find a prostitute in Williamsburg. Over the course of the eighteenth century, however, prostitution was firmly established in American cities. An instance from New York in 1793 may illustrate this, while also showing that the prostitution sub-culture was not yet so clearly defined as to prevent misunderstandings. Harry Bedlow, a gentleman calling himself "Lawyer Smith", met a seventeen-year-old seamstress called Lanah Sawyer. He walked out with her for several evenings, before taking her to a bawdy house and having sex. She accused him of rape, but he was acquitted, on the strength of his lawyer's argument that a working woman could not possibly "imagine that a man of his situation would pay her any attention . . . unless with a view of promoting illicit commerce." In the riot of working men that followed this judgment, brothels were among the objects of attack.

In the words of John D'Emilio and Estelle B. Freedman, in the nineteenth century "sexual services became one of women's labours to be drawn outside of the home and into the public sphere of commerce." In 1858, William W. Sanger, resident physician at Blackwell's Island, New York City, estimated a minimum of six thousand prostitutes in New York, one to every sixty-four men, and the picture was much the same in other urban centres. Of the two thousand women questioned by Sanger, 933 had been servants,

499 had lived at home with their parents or friends, and the rest had been scraping a living at sweatshop trades as tailoresses, hat-trimmers, flower-makers and the like. One of Sanger's questions was "What was the cause of your becoming a prostitute?", and the answers are interesting. The results were:

Destitution	525
Inclination	513
Seduced and abandoned	258
Drink, and the desire to drink	181
Ill-treatment of parents, relative, or husbands	164
As an easy life	124
Bad company	84
Persuaded by prostitutes	71
Too idle to work	29
Violated	27
Seduced on board emigrant ships	16
Seduced in emigrant boarding-houses	8

It will be seen that while "destitution" was clearly the chief cause, one way or another, of entry into prostitution, over a quarter of those surveyed claim to have become prostitutes through "inclination". Being conned or forced into prostitution by a pimp does not feature in this list, nor does being tricked into a brothel and forced to work. There is some evidence that the latter did happen, and that girls inveigled into entering brothels had to make the best of their situation once there. Barbara Meil Hobson quotes a case from the Suffolk County Superior Court in 1863. Mary Clark, a prostitute, testifying against Fanny Moore, a prostitute charged with robbery, said:

> I am seventeen years of age. I came to the city a fortnight ago before from Lowell. I was brought here by Fanny who persuaded me to come here to work saying that she kept a shop. I did not know what sort of house I was coming to.

This sort of sexual slavery was institutionalised on the Barbary Coast, where Chinese girls were imported, often with false promises of marriage, or having been kidnapped from or sold by their families, and were put to work as prostitutes in cheap cribs, one-room brothels of the lowest kind. D'Emilio and Freedman note that, "At the peak of importation during the 1870s, the census listed 'prostitute' as the occupation of two-thirds of the

ANONYMOUS PHOTOGRAPH: *A girl in a Mexican bordello, 1900-15*

thirty-five hundred Chinese women in California." Throughout the century, it was new waves of immigrants, especially the Irish, who supplied the new generations of prostitutes.

ANONYMOUS PHOTOGRAPH:
A woman in a Chinese bagnio, San Francisco, 19th century

At first the South – with its own distinctive pattern of sexual abuse of slaves – lagged behind the North in the commercialisation of sex, but the Civil War, with its attendant poverty, caused a prostitution boom. One soldier stationed in Richmond, Virginia, wrote home that the women "damnyankee us on the street in the daytime, but at night the skirts come up for good yankee gold." The opening up of the West, when the inhabitants of cattle and mining towns were largely single men, was another strong element in the development of prostitution in the United States.

By the turn of the present century, public concern about the "social evil" of prostitution was so intense that at least thirty-five cities and states launched major investigations into the problem. Such moral fervour was of course not new. It can be traced back to Cotton Mather, and had appeared earlier in such reforming projects as the Penitent Females' Refuge founded in 1822 by the Female Missionary Society, which offered a secluded refuge to penitent prostitutes. In Boston in 1825, moral and religious agitation over the preceding years reached a peak, and outrage spilled over into violence in a manner strikingly reminiscent of the "rough music" with which English villagers signalled their disapproval of sexual misbehaviour. The first brothel to be attacked was the Beehive, run by a widow known as Marm

Cooper on North Margin Street, after which a mob three hundred strong rioted for three days. They were disguised in blackface, and carried pitchforks, tin cans, drums and whistles.

The turn-of-the-century moral agitation, however, was orchestrated. It was largely fuelled by fears about the White Slave Trade, which were stirred up by sensationalist literature published by reforming organisations. One of the best accounts of American prostitution, the autobiography of an anonymous prostitute known only as Madeleine, was written and published as a deliberate counter to such propaganda, in an attempt to convey the reality of prostitutes' lives to a public whose concern was being informed by fantasy.

Madeleine: An Autobiography was first published in 1919. White-slavery, she insisted, was a fiction. She had met every kind of prostitute working for every kind of reason, except "the pure girl who had been trapped and violated and sold into slavery". Her own story was much more interesting. Madeleine was born and raised in a small town in the Mid-West. Her parents were pious and educated, and she was one of a large and happy family. But during her childhood her father became an alcoholic, and turned violent, often subjecting her to unexplained and vicious whippings. The family sank into poverty.

When she was thirteen, Madeleine's family moved "to the worst neighbourhood in the town. On either side of us, and across the street, the houses were occupied by prostitutes." These neighbours were ostensibly running boarding-houses, or working as dressmakers or laundresses; in addition, the wives of the working-men of the district supplemented the family finances by prostitution. Madeleine quickly learned to compare their living standards with her own: "These people had good things to eat, served on nice china. They had clean table-cloths; we had none at all. Their houses were palaces compared with the wretched place that I called home."

Before she was seventeen, influenced by such companions, and with a strong "mating instinct", Madeleine lost her virginity. This was sometime in the 1880s. She then left home to work in a St Louis factory, meaning to send money back to her family, but soon discovered she was pregnant. Reduced to penury, she became a streetwalker. She contracted a venereal disease, and in hospital was put in a ward with a more practised prostitute, Mamie, from whose coarse conversation she at first shrunk, but whose "spontaneous good nature" was proof against all Madeleine's refined distaste. Mamie advised her when she was well to enter a house.

Madeleine joined Mamie in Miss Laura's Kansas City brothel. There were eleven other girls. Miss Laura's was one of three high-class houses in Kansas City, which also supported many less salubrious establishments. Laura – herself an ex-prostitute, as were most madams – was a kind and fair boss, to whom it was "a far more important matter that the girls should look upon the place as 'home' than that she should make a great deal of money."

"Parlor hours" were from 8 p.m. to 4 a.m. The girls had to pay half the standard charges to the house, but could keep any gratuities; the first ten dollars earned each week went to pay for board. There was no system of petty fines as in other houses, except for failing to attend throughout working hours. The chief source of income for the house was from the liquor which the girls persuaded their clients to buy.

Madeleine's early weeks at Miss Laura's were an unmitigated disaster. She was rude and unresponsive with the customers, and so inexperienced that several times she was bilked of her fee. She was amazed that the other girls were constantly making or buying little things for her forthcoming baby: they "were as interested in the coming event as the most normal feminine household would have been". It was not unusual to continue working during pregnancy; some prostitutes reported a rise in custom.

Madeleine's baby died at birth. She resolved to leave the life, and after first visiting her family went to Chicago in search of work, which she found in a department store. But when a desperate letter arrived from her mother telling her that she was being separated from the children and consigned to the poorhouse, Madeleine threw up her job and entered a Chicago brothel, "one of the most notorious joints in the United States", telling her mother that she had had a rise in salary in order to explain the extra money she was now able to send.

On her first evening in this new place, she was expected to take part in a public exhibition as part of an orgy for a group of regular clients. She offended all the other girls, and the Madam, by refusing to do so, making it clear that she thought herself a cut above them. Breakfast was not a comfortable meal:

> "What do you think of this one, girls? She don't know she's a whore. She thinks she's a lady!"
>
> "Sure she does. The poor fool don't know that men come here because they've got ladies at home and they like the change."

WILLIAM GLACKENS: *Interior, 1899*

Madeleine writes, "At Miss Laura's my chief aversion had been the physical contact with men. In this place it was the contact with the women of the house that I loathed." In turn, the girls of the house, who were uneducated and coarse but clearly vital and full of their own rather bitter humour, spared no effort in shocking someone they must have seen as a Goody-Two-Shoes with talk "about their bedfellows of the night before, given with the most minute detail, particularly of abhorrent perversions". Nevertheless, Madeleine was financially successful in this house, largely it seems because the clients were attracted by her submissive and innocent little-girl air.

Her next move was to a "swell house", also in Chicago, run by an icy, "severely corseted" lady known as Miss Allen. Everything here was conducted with decorum and style. The girls of the house were "haughty dames who possessed a dozen evening gowns and kept their own maids". Here Madeleine stayed, off and on, for five years. But as she soon had a baby son to support, and expenses at Miss Allen's were high, she also worked elsewhere, notably in Winnipeg, where she was "the most sought-after girl in town". She had begun to enjoy her work, experiencing "a glad response" to her clients. Despite being parted from her baby, "I was happy".

Another realm of prostitution into which she ventured was that of the occasional or clandestine prostitute: respectable women who had not given up their place in society could still sell themselves at houses of assignation. Madeleine worked in such a house with a girl who was a student at the Chicago Conservatory of Music. "She was engaged to a rising young lawyer in the Western state from which she came, and she had deliberately chosen this means of earning money for her trousseau." As Madeleine notes, with a hint of bitterness:

> This man, to whom she was afterward married, rose to a high position in the affairs of the nation, and she, his wife, became famous for her political acumen and her social graces. Society placed no scarlet brand upon her nor upon her kind.

Numbers of students at the Conservatory and the Art Institute worked at this particular house, together with married women who either "sat for company" or were "on call".

Madeleine's son died in infancy. She was pregnant again with twins, but in her grief procured an abortion which nearly killed her. At twenty-two, there seemed nothing to live for. In particular, she developed a hatred of men, asking, "What does any man know of anything but sexual gratification?" But

ANONYMOUS PHOTOGRAPH: *Creede parlor-house, Creede, Colorado, 1892*

she went back to work at Miss Allen's, where her best friend Olga rebuked her: "If there is anything out of place under the sun, it's a prostitute who hates men."

Madeleine had in fact been conducting an on-off love affair throughout her life as a prostitute with a mining engineer named Paul Martin from Butte, Montana, and at this point she set off to join him. In Butte she first came across the seamier side of her profession. There were only two first-class houses, together with variety shows and dance halls, but most of the prostitutes were "crib" girls who sold themselves many times a day for a pittance, working from makeshift open shacks. In one of these, Madeleine found a girl, Norma, who had previously been a "star boarder" at Miss Allen's, and was now charging a dollar a time. She had been consigned to the cribs by her pimp, a gambler; most of the crib girls were supporting pimps, who would not be tolerated in a parlor-house. She warned Madeleine: "It's a tough game in this town. The girls in the big houses are all hundreds of dollars in debt, with no chance to get out." The red-light district of Butte was Park Street, and as Anne M. Butler shows in her study *Daughters of Joy, Sisters of Misery: Prostitutes in the American West 1865-90*, it was noted for its poverty, filth and violence. While the crib girls were spared the many expenses of the parlor-house prostitutes, they were still caught in a poverty-trap, despite being able to swell their takings by the illegal sale of liquor. Paradoxically, the rent for a crib was greater than that for a place in a brothel. Anne Butler gives an instance from Boise, Idaho, where Agnes Bush ran both a parlor-house and cribs in a back alley. Prostitutes in the house paid $20 a month in rent, while those in the squalid cribs paid $48 to $60.

At the age of twenty-eight, contrary to the popularly-accepted pattern of a prostitute's career, which had her inevitably sinking to the lowest level before succumbing to drink and disease, Madeleine had reached the prosperous top of her profession, and opened her own house in a town in the Canadian Northwest. Rejecting the numerous drink-sodden women who attempted to enlist in the operation, "I sent down into the States after three girls that I knew, attractive girls, not overly given to the use of liquor; and late in November I opened my place of business." It was an instant success:

> As soon as it was dark the men began to arrive, in buggies and in hacks, in hotel buses, on horseback, and afoot – all sorts and conditions, gentlemen, hoodlums, and the gradations between. There were railroad men and back officials, cowpunchers and professional men, wheat-growers and business men, Mounted Police in mufti, bartenders, clerks, and most of the male choir members of the English church.

Working flat-out from dusk till dawn, the girls still failed to accommodate all the hopeful customers. By the end of her first summer, "my bank-account had swollen to a size that was far beyond my wildest expectations."

After a couple of years of prosperity, Madeleine became an alcoholic; in saving herself from that, she also abandoned prostitution, giving over her house to Mildred, her deputy. She became once again a respectable woman, who put her career on record largely, it seems, to counter the "white-slavery" scares which were widely believed in the early years of the century.

It has seemed worthwhile following Madeleine's career in detail both because it is a rare first-hand account, but also because her experiences embraced such a wide range of types of prostitution. This does not seem unusual (a modern comparison might be the very varied career of Dolores French), and as Ruth Rosen shows in her book *The Lost Sisterhood: Prostitution in America, 1900-1918*, Madeleine's restless moving from house to house is typical of the period.

What is perhaps most valuable in Madeleine's book, apart from the sense

WILLIAM GLACKENS: *Chez Mouquin (New York City), 1905*

we gain of her as an individual human being with complex, divided emotions, is her very cool-headed exposition of the household economy of the brothel, from the high-class house catering for the well-to-do, to the parlor-house catering for the working man, to the squalor of the cribs, and, below them, the street. It is clear that, as in every business, the manufacture and sale of the product is only the visible tip of the organisational effort required to make the finances work. While Madeleine felt ashamed of selling herself, she felt proud of being paid. She earned her independence, and turned into a shrewd businesswoman.

In terms which are echoed by today's feminists, as well as voiced by such contemporary thinkers as Emma Goldman, Madeleine contrasts the honesty of the prostitute's sexual transaction with that of the wife. Prostitutes, she writes, "differ in only one respect from the women who sell themselves into unloved and often loathsome marriage – they do not cheat in the delivery of the merchandise for which they are paid."

In 1912, George J. Kneeland conducted a thorough survey of prostitution in New York City. He found prostitutes working in brothels, tenement house apartments, furnished room houses, disorderly hotels and massage parlors, as well as in the back rooms of saloons, on excursion boats and in amusement parks, with strong connections to "restaurants, pool rooms, delicatessen stores, candy shops, hair dressing and manicure parlors, barber shops, cigar stores, palmist and clairvoyant parlors, livery stables, and opium dens". In addition, prostitution, which had been largely a female-run business, was now dominated by men, who creamed off the profits of this vast trade.

Kneeland estimated over 300 massage parlors, which were a cover for prostitution, 112 furnished room assignation houses, 90 disorderly hotels, 1172 "vice resorts" in 575 tenement houses, and visited 142 brothels or "parlor-houses" in Manhattan. Of these, twenty were 50-cent houses, eighty were $1.00 houses, six were $2.00 houses, thirty-four were $5.00 or $10.00 houses, and for two – presumably at the very top end of the scale – no prices were known. These more exclusive houses were very luxuriously appointed and well-run, and made a speciality of "circuses" or live sex shows, for which men were known to pay $50-$75. At the bottom end of the scale was the 50-cent house:

> In one of the houses of this type of wooden bench was placed against the wall of the receiving parlor. Business was very brisk at the time the investigator entered. The bench was full of customers crowded close

together, while others, who could not be accommodated with seats, stood about the room. At the foot of the stairs which led to the bedrooms above, a man was stationed. Every time a visitor came groping his way down the stairs, the businesslike and aggressive announcer would cry out, "Next!"

Kneeland obtained a number of the cards which were alloted to each girl in such a house, to be stamped with a hole representing each client. For instance, of sixteen cards from a "notorious one-dollar house on West 28th Street", the largest number of holes punched on 9 July 1912 was thirty. This level of business is supported by other evidence. The Vice Commission in Chicago found an average of 15 clients a day for 18 inmates in one house in a period covering 22 months. A record of the clients entertained by the girls over five days' business in a similar Chicago house was presented to the court at the trial of a brothel-keeper in 1911. It ran:

	Sunday	Monday	Tuesday	Wednesday	Thursday
Alice	20	16	11	15	–
Vere	16	17	14	16	–
Kitty	24	14	12	9	17
Mina	36	22	12	10	–
Edith	11	15	15	4	–
Florince	20	23	21	21	45
Sophy	–	–	18	21	–
Annie	–	–	–	–	22

It is interesting to note that only two girls worked all five days, and that one worked only two and another only one day. There is also a clear pattern of popularity among the girls. In four nights Edith had only 45 customers, while over five nights Florince served 130. Wednesday and Thursday, when the clients' pay was nearly spent, were clearly slack nights. The two busiest nights of the week, Friday and Saturday, are unfortunately not recorded. It was not unknown for girls in such houses to entertain more than sixty men in a night.

The customers for these different levels of parlor-house were, of course, differentiated by class and income. The 50-cent houses catered for "long-shoremen, truck drivers, street cleaners, coal heavers, soldiers and sailors, recently landed immigrants of low moral standards, and labourers of all kinds". The $1.00 and $2.00 houses served "proprietors of small business enterprises, clerks, bookkeepers, bartenders, barbers, tailors, waiters, sol-diers, sailors, messengers in banks, members of social and political clubs or of benefit organisations". The highest priced houses, on the other hand, were patronised by "prominent customers":

> One such individual is the New York agent for a famous automobile concern; another is the manager of a company which manufactures a well-known typewriter; another travels about from city to city selling hats; while still a fourth is connected with a celebrated watch company.

The owners of the parlor-houses fought a running battle against less organised levels of prostitution, doing everything in their power "to undermine the business done by women on the street, in flats and in massage parlors". They would for instance act as police informants, while remaining relatively free from harassment – except during major crack-downs – because of the large sums of money spent on police bribes. One police officer arrived at a brothel while an investigator was there and asked to see the owner, with the words, "I'm broke. He hasn't seen me for a few nights and I would like some sugar."

Even so, street prostitutes could make a better living at prostitution than any other trade open to them. Kneeland managed to get one young "poorly dressed, rather ignorant and unsophisticated street walker" to keep a diary. In 32 days she earned $211, averaging between $6.00 and $7.00 a day (at a dollar a time). As a domestic servant she would have been paid about $23.00 a month plus board and lodging, as a factory girl roughly the same, and as a shop girl slightly more. In other words she was earning roughly ten times what she could have done elsewhere. No wonder one Illinois prostitute told their Vice Committee, "I'll live fast and die early rather than become somebody's kitchen slave. Restaurant work is bad enough, but I won't be a dog in anybody's kitchen."

Many girls went on the streets because it was "easier" than any alternative employment. One told Kneeland, echoing her Illinois sister, that she was tired of the drudgery of domestic service: "I'd rather do this than be kicked around like a dog in a kitchen by some woman who calls herself a lady." Another told him she went on the game because "I loved the excitement and a good time, easy money and good clothes." A third simply told him, "I was born bad and actually enjoy the life."

Most prostitutes were aged 18-25. Barbara Meil Hobson notes:

> That prostitutes often retired by the age of twenty-five suggests that prostitution was a transitory phase in the lives of women . . . The age at which most prostitutes abandoned their trade was the age at which most women married.

ANONYMOUS PHOTOGRAPH: *A girl in a Mexican bordello, 1900-15*

Of all the red-light districts of America, the one which has the most distinct importance is Storyville in New Orleans, which was an experiment in the containment and regulation of prostitution lasting from 1 January 1898 until the fall of 1917, when Storyville was closed on the orders of the US Navy because of its alleged threat to the morals and health of sailors at

55

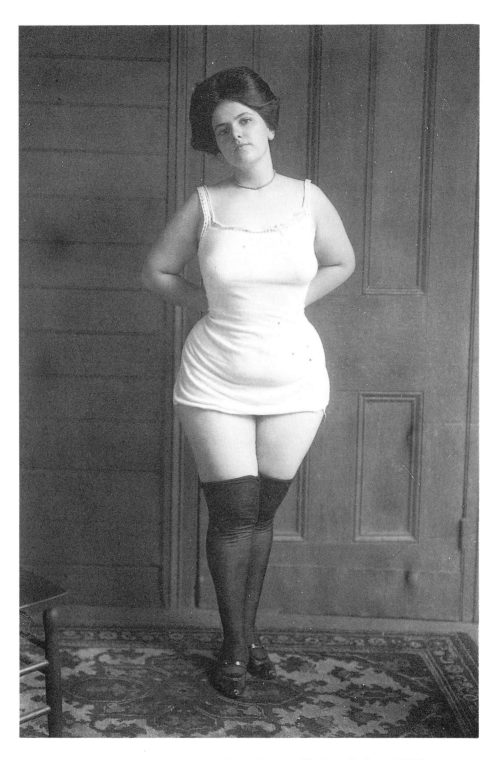

E.J. BELLOCQ: *A woman in a Storyville brothel, c. 1912*

the New Orleans base. The area was naughtily named Storyville by the press, after the reforming Alderman Sidney Story, but its own denizens called it simply "the District".

New Orleans had a long history of prostitution, documented in Herbert Asbury's *The French Quarter*, beginning in the seventeenth century with the arrival of shiploads of French prostitutes who had been arrested and deported to populate France's foreign colonies. By the end of the nineteenth century, the reputation of New Orleans as a seething centre of vice made the authorities search desperately for a new answer to an old problem, and the result was Story's creation of a discrete and tolerated – though still technically illegal – prostitution district.

Over the next twenty years, Storyville was to be the cradle of a new art, which, in marrying European traditions of harmony to an African melodic and rhythmic legacy, changed the course of twentieth-century music: jazz. Key figures in the early development of jazz, such as Tony Johnson and Jelly Roll Morton, worked as pianists and singers in the Storyville brothels, where they were known as "professors". Jelly Roll Morton, talking to his biographer Alan Lomax, gave a lively picture of the Storyville scene:

> They had everything in the District from the highest class to the lowest – creep joints where they'd put the feelers on a guy's clothes, cribs that rented for about five dollars a day and had just about room enough for a bed, small-time houses where the price was from fifty cents to a dollar and they put on naked dances, circuses, and jive. Then, of course, we had the mansions where everything was of the very highest class. These houses were filled up with the most expensive furniture and paintings. Three of them had mirror parlors where you couldn't find the door for the mirrors, the one at Lula White's costing $30,000. Mirrors stood at the foot and head of all the beds. It was in these mansions that the best of the piano players worked.

Josie Arlington's mansion, for instance, advertised itself as "Absolutely and unquestionably the most decorative and costly fitted-out sporting palace ever placed before the American public", though Josie herself was remembered by a rival madam simply as a "loud-mouthed, low-class woman, but pretentious".

Al Rose's reconstruction of this world in his book *Storyville, New Orleans* mixes musicology, historical research and oral history to build up a composite account of life in the District. He gives a splendid list of names of Storyville characters compiled by musician Danny Barker, which gives some of the flavour of the place:

Flamin' Mamie, Crying Emma, Bucktown Bessie, Dirty Dog, Steel Arm Johnny, Mary Meathouse, Gold Tooth Gussie, Big Butt Annie, Naked Mouf Mattie, Bird Leg Nora, Bang Zang, Boxcar Shorty, Sneaky Pete, Titanic, Coke Eyed Laura, Yellow Gal, Black Sis, Boar Hog, Yard Dog, Bodiddly, Roody Doody, Big Bull Cora, Piggy, Big Piggy, Stingaree, Bull Frog Sonny, Toot Nan, Knock on the Wall, Sore Dick, Sugar Pie, Cherry Red, Buck Tooth Rena, Bad Blood, Copper Wire, Snaggle Mouf Mary, Linker-top, Topsy, Scratch, Joe the Pimp, Onery Bob, TeeTee, Tee Nome, Tee Share, Tee Boy, Taw Head, Smoke Stack, Stack O Dollars, Pupsy, Boogers, Copper Cent, Street Rabbit, BooBoo, Big BooBoo, Fast Black, Eight Ball, Lily the Crip, Tenderloin Thelma, Three Finger Annie, Charlie Bow Wow, Good Lord the Lifter, Peachanno, Cold Blooded Carrie, Miss Thing, Jack the Bear.

The brothel life of this colourful milieu was recorded for posterity by a local photographer, E.J. Bellocq, Storyville's Toulouse-Lautrec, whose work in turn provided the inspiration for Louis Malle's film *Pretty Baby*. Al Rose interviewed Violet, a real "pretty baby", who was active as a child prostitute before the close of Storyville in 1917, often working with her mother as one of over fifty such "mother and daughter combinations" in the District. She was born in 1904, and says, "I was a 'trick' baby. That means my father was one of the johns that paid my mother for a fuck." Describing growing up in a brothel, she describes the natural transition from witness to participant in the business of the house:

> One time Cora one of the girls had a john and she was sucking him off. It was nothing new to me, I seen it plenty of times before but only lately I'd be in the room while they were doing it. I said "I can do that." So we took turns . . . Then he fucked her while I felt his balls . . . I made five dollars for my end of that one, and then I started turning tricks myself just by blowing. I was still only ten years old and not very big so I didn't fuck. It was two years more before I did that. So I was a virgin for two years.

Her virginity was auctioned to the highest bidder in one of madam Emma Johnson's famous "circuses". She recalls, "My mother was in the circus, too. She's the one who used to fuck the pony."

This account of an abused and despoiled childhood has, in fact, an oddly innocent and happy air, and by no means the ending in degradation and misery that one might expect. For Violet married an ex-customer in 1921, raised three daughters and a son in respectable contentment, and remembered her unusual upbringing without bitterness or unhappiness: "to me it

ANONYMOUS PHOTOGRAPH: *A girl in a Mexican bordello, 1900-15*

seems just like anything else – like a kid whose father owns a grocery store. He helps him in the store. Well, my mother didn't sell groceries."

Prostitution in the United States has developed along fairly predictable lines in the twentieth century. The three most distinctive features have perhaps been the emergence of the call-girl and the rise of the massage parlor, both of which methods of prostitution have encouraged a better educated, more independent and more middle-class type of prostitute. Also significant – although perhaps not quite so important as the enormous amount of attention which has been accorded it – has been the State of Nevada's experiment with legalised brothels such as the notorious Mustang Ranch.

Two books which appeared in 1958 neatly summarise the old and the new in American prostitution. Dr Harold Greenwald's *The Call Girl: A Social and Psychoanalytic Study* described New York City's prostitutes as earning untaxed incomes of about $20,000 a year, charging $20-$100 a session. *Cast the First Stone*, co-written by Sara Harris and John M. Murtagh, Chief Magistrate of the City of New York, described the sordid street trade which has always co-existed with the brothel and the courtesan. Among the principal streetwalking areas was Coney Island, where a mixture of teen-agers and women in their fifties and sixties did a thriving trade under the boardwalk with the area's teeming pleasure-seekers. Competition kept prices low, and the women also resented "too many freebies around wanting to give it away". The older women, Murtagh and Harris report, took on "many men" for fifty cents apiece, "any way you want it". The teenagers could charge more, from $2 to $10 a time, but even they, the authors estimate, serviced between twenty and thirty men a day.

The invention of the telephone is the foundation of the profession of call-girl, though similar arrangements, with a central message service which took orders and relayed them to outworkers, had existed previously. Sidney Biddle Barrows, the so-called "Mayflower Madam", ran for five years until she was arrested in 1984 a high-class Manhattan call-girl operation called Cachet. Her idea, after working as a phone girl at another escort agency, was to create a "successful, elegant, honest, and fun" operation which would provide a superior service to clients and, most importantly, support rather than exploit the women who worked for it. For call-girls at this level, the credit card portaprinter is probably their most vital piece of equipment.

The Nevada brothels are run along similarly business-like lines. In 1973, Nevada had 33 brothels (all but two run by women) with between 225 and 250 women working in them, with an average of five girls per town brothel and seven girls per rural brothel, although the largest, the Mustang Ranch, had over fifty girls working there. This outfit was owned and run by Joe Conforte, a man with an early career in petty crime, and a prison record for attempted extortion. At the Mustang, the girls worked for a minimum of three weeks without a break, and had to earn a minimum of $1000 a week in summer and $500 in winter to stay. They worked a 14-16 hour day, three weeks on, one week off. Their cut was 50%, reduced to about 40% by the deduction of 10% of the take up to $10 for room and board, $1 a day for the night maid, $1 for the cashier, $1 for each pair of panties washed, $2 for each house-gown washed and $20 for a weekly medical plus the cost of any prescriptions.

For some, the safety and legality of these brothels, and the undoubted opportunity to make a lot of money very quickly, outweighs the prison-like atmosphere caused by their isolation and their high fences, and the stressful working conditions. Women may stay in the same house for years, but for most the Nevada brothels are a short-term solution to financial problems. Records for seventy-seven girls in 1973 showed that twenty worked ten days or less before quitting, and forty-five worked less than a month. On the other hand, some had worked as long as four years in the same house.

Certainly, working in brothels or for escort agencies is much safer than the streets, for the client can be checked out, and traced if need be. Streetwalkers are also much more vulnerable to police harassment and arrest, and are able to charge only a fraction of call-girl rates. While Sidney Biddle Barrows's Cachet was charging $125 an hour, streetwalkers on Manhattan's Lower East Side were charging $10 for oral sex, and $10-$20 for sexual intercourse.

Still, there is money to be made even on the street, and escort agencies, massage parlors, and brothels are all highly profitable businesses even if, as Sydney Biddle Barrows found, they also carry risks. Because these businesses, while they may have respectable fronts, are essentially offering illegal services, it is impossible to make even a guess at the value of their combined annual turnover, but it must be huge. The annual turnover of the legal Mustang Ranch is in the region of $5 million. Similarly there is no reliable figure for the number of prostitutes currently working in the United States: informed guesswork from prostitutes' organisations puts the figure at between one and one-and-a-half million.

4 THEY ORDER THESE THINGS
BETTER IN FRANCE

PROSTITUTION IN EUROPE

The French being the French, we have copious, indeed superabundant, records of prostitution in France reaching back to medieval times, which can serve as a model for the rest of continental Europe. Prostitution throughout medieval Europe, except in its most casual forms, was closely linked to and supervised by the church and state, and an interesting story can be made of the fluctuating attitudes to the "daughters of joy", who were alternately punished and taxed depending on the mood of the times.

As Jacques Rossiaud puts it in his study of medieval prostitution in Dijon:

> The city fathers who organized the brothels and recruited the prostitutes, knew well that they were taking poor girls driven by violence or by poverty and subjecting them to the sin of lust. They might have asked themselves if they were not thus accomplices to public crimes. But they also knew that the city whose fortunes were safeguarded was producing nuns as well as whores. They themselves presided over this dual process. In order to marry some of their daughters, they made eternal virgins of others by inducing them to live in community as a lay nun in a *béguinage*, to serve in the hospitals, or to lead a life of prayer in the cloister. Two groups of women – the only women who had a collective identity – coexisted in any city worthy of the name: nuns and whores. If the prostitutes were crushed by the vice of lust, the nuns were equally crushed by the virtue of chastity, for everyone thought that virginity could be maintained only at the price of inhuman suffering.

One of the most noteworthy aspects of medieval prostitution is the way it intertwines with the religious life. Brothel-keepers were known as the "Abbess" or "Abbot". Most remarkable of all, in Albi in 1526 the entire community of the municipal brothel, growing too old to profitably carry on their original profession, entered the religious life, turning brothel to nunnery at one stroke. Most cities contained a community of repentant sisters, in what Leah Lydia Otis calls "the logical charitable complement of

ANONYMOUS WOODCUT: *German brothel, 15th century*

the municipally authorised brothel." Most bordellos were run by women; seventy-five out of eighty-three cases in Dijon, for instance.

Rossiaud says that clergy made up twenty per cent of the clientele of the bathhouses and private bordellos of Dijon. As the French vagabond poet François Villon put it (in Galway Kinnell's masterly translation):

> At the Celestines and Carthusians.
> Although they lead the narrow life
> Between them have a large provision
> Of what these girls are starving for,
> Just ask Jacqueline or Perette
> Or Isabelle who comments, "Great!"
> Seeing they're in such a state
> You probably won't go to Hell for it.

Villon, who was born in Paris in 1431, is the great poet of whoredom. The very smell of the small Parisian brothel where the poet and his prostitute mistress lived as "bad rat bad cat" is summoned up in the coarse exuberance of his "Ballade of Fat Margot":

Then we make peace and she lets me a big fart
Puffed up worse than a poisonous dung-beetle,
Laughing, she sits her fist on my crown,
"Baby," she says and whacks my tail,
The two of us dead drunk we sleep like a top
And when we wake and her belly cries
She climbs aboard so as not to spoil her fruit,
I groan underneath, pressed flatter than a plank,
As she wipes out all the lechery in me
In this whorehouse where we hold our state.

One can imagine this scene in one of the Paris buildings described by Jacques de Vitry two centuries earlier, which housed "a college upstairs and a brothel downstairs".

The development of prostitution in continental Europe parallels that in Britain. Certain cities, such as Venice and Paris, were renowned as centres of vice, but most towns and cities had established prostitution districts, and rural prostitution existed in its more casual and domestic forms. The great explosion of prostitution which came with the industrial revolution swept the continent as it did Britain, and gave rise to the first scientific study of the problem, *La Prostitution dans la Ville de Paris* by A.J.B. Parent-Duchatelet.

Basing his studies on 42,699 prostitutes officially registered by the Paris authorities in 1832, Parent-Duchatelet produced an exhaustive study, right down to a famously irrelevant chart classifying them by hair, eye and eyebrow colour. The result of his work, writes Jill Harsin, was to transform "the *fille de joie* to a member of the urban proletariat". The chief cause of prostitution, he showed, was not vice but lack of work and poverty.

Starting out strongly disapproving of the wickedness of prostitutes, Parent-Duchatelet inexorably came to pity and in some ways admire them. He notes for instance that many of them were fond of reading, and writes:

> Their reading is always of histories and novels, particularly those which describe tragic scenes which excite strong emotions; but what seems strange, is that one never finds in their hands licentious or obscene books.

Other popular pastimes were dancing, cards, needlework and music.

Regarding prostitution as "inevitable", Parent-Duchatelet strongly supported a system of regulation which would take girls off the streets and into legally and medically supervised brothels, the *maisons de tolérance* or *maisons closes*. These officially tolerated brothels were only abolished in 1946.

We know a good deal about life in the *maisons closes*. The painter Henri de Toulouse-Lautrec lived in one at no. 6, rue des Moulins, and depicted its inhabitants in many drawings and paintings of their daily routine. Brothels such as the Chabanais, known as the House of All Nations, with its magnificent décor (the Moorish room was particularly admired) and sumptuous fittings (including a red copper tub for champagne baths), attracted royalty and writers. Meaner establishments existed to cater for all the gradations of society.

It was largely because of the luxury of the great Parisian brothels, rather than any greater ease in finding prostitutes there, that Paris became in the nineteenth century such a strong focus of illicit desire, particularly to the English. Even so upright a figure as Charles Dickens allowed himself to be excited, and perhaps more, by the *lorettes* he saw in Paris with his louche friend Wilkie Collins, with whom he indulged in what he called "Haroun Alraschid expeditions". For most Englishmen a visit to Paris was the frank excuse for a debauch.

A particular feature of the Paris brothels was their sex shows or circuses. These featured simulated lesbian scenes, often enacted by girls who were themselves lesbians (who were preferred by many brothel-keepers as being quieter and less trouble than heterosexual prostitutes; many of the brothels also catered for a lesbian clientele). Many brothels also featured shows in which a woman had sex with a dog, the grander brothels favouring Great Danes and the suburban ones, Newfoundlands. When Walter came into a legacy, "I went first to Paris, where I ran a course of bawdy house amusements, saw a big dog fuck a woman who turned her rump towards it as if she were a bitch."

Another attraction for the English traveller was the ready availability of fellatio, which is still known by prostitutes throughout the world as "french"; Walter noted that French women "do it as a matter of course, either as a preliminary or finish". Anal intercourse, too, was universally practised in the brothels, where it was known as "turning the medal" (perhaps, in English, "the other side of the coin"). Street girls, we are told by Fiaux, a man whose disgust at such practices was equalled only by his fascination, refused any requests for this, telling clients, "There are women for that!" Interestingly, it is known now as "greek", an appellation which recalls the evidence of Greek vase-painting that this was the preferred intercourse of prostitutes in ancient Greece, perhaps as a contraceptive measure. Aristophanes confirms that it was the usual practice of Corinthian prostitutes, and Sir Kenneth Dover remarks that, " 'Corinth' had something of the same connotations for an Athenian as 'Paris' for a nineteenth-century Englishman."

In 1880 the novelist Emile Zola published his novel *Nana*, set in the 1860s during the decadence of the Second Empire, which traced the life of a prostitute in unparalleled detail. The theme of the book, Zola wrote, was simple: "A whole society hurling itself at the cunt. A pack of hounds after a bitch, who is not even on heat and makes fun of the hounds following her." It portrays, in rich, vivid detail, a world in which, "From the top of the social ladder to the bottom, everybody was at it!" Zola's research for this powerful and voluptuous work included a visit to the house of the cultured and intelligent courtesan Madame Valtesse de la Bigne, the luxurious interior of which is reflected in Nana's home:

> The company went upstairs to take coffee in the little drawing-room, where a couple of lamps shed a soft glow over the pink hangings and lacquer and old gold of the knick-knacks. At that hour of the evening the light played discreetly over coffers, bronzes and china, lighting up silver and ivory inlaid work, picking out the shining contours of a carved stick, and covering a panel with the shimmering gleams of watered silk. The fire, which had been burning since the afternoon, was dying out in glowing embers. It was very warm, and the air between the curtains and the door-hangings was hot and languid. The room was full of Nana's intimate life: a pair of her gloves, a fallen handkerchief, an open book lay scattered about, evoking an impression of their owner *en déshabillé*, in the midst of her scent of violets and that happy-go-lucky untidiness which created such a charming effect in these rich surroundings.

This is the world of *demi-mondaines* such as Cora Pearl, who appears in the novel as Lucy Stewart, but Zola also explores the world of the streetwalker and the oppressive morals police, and, in the relationship of Nana and the streetwalker Satin, captures the lesbian resonances of many relationships between prostitutes.

For a contrast to Zola's account of fashionable Parisian prostitution, one need look no further than Guy de Maupassant's marvellous short story "La Maison Tellier", which depicts a small brothel in Normandy, where, he explains, "The stigma attached to prostitution, so deep and inveterate in big towns, does not exist . . . The peasant says: 'It's a good trade.' " His fictional house remains the pattern of many brothels in rural France today:

JEAN BERAUD: *Dinner at the Ambassadeurs, late 19th century*

The house had two entrances. On the corner there was a sort of shady café which was open in the evening to workmen and sailors. Two of the young women engaged in the principal occupation of the establishment were detailed to minister to the needs of this section of the clientele . . .

The other three ladies (there were only five in all) formed a sort of aristocracy and were reserved for the company on the first floor, except when the first-floor room was deserted and they were needed downstairs.

A more modern account of such a house is in Jeanne Cordelier's autobiography, *The Life*. After working at the most sordid end of Parisian prostitution in areas such as the notorious rue St Denis, Jeanne ended up in a bar in

Cuers, Provence, in the 1960s. The price was twenty-five francs a time, of which half went to her and half to the bar. A diary entry depicts a typical Saturday night:

> Two-thirty: seventy-five customers. I'd never have believed it. Especially in what Toudé made me buy – a brown jersey dress from Ted Lapidus that's as draggy as a sleepless night. This dress cost me a weekend's take – too tired to figure it out exactly.

The best picture of prostitution in France in the 1970s is contained in Allan Mankoff's user's guide to the European sex industry, *Mankoff's Lusty Europe*. This very thoroughly researched volume can be taken as a trust-worthy guide to prices, places and pleasures, though some embarrassment may follow for anyone who acts on Mankoff's maxim that, "in Paris it is often axiomatic that the less likely the girl appears to be, the more likely she is." Brothels, Mankoff reports, were, though illegal, still easily found. Their trade, however, was in competition with such modern refinements as the motorised prostitutes who cruise the circle round the Etoile, the girls (and, increasingly, transsexuals) who service customers in the backs of cars in the Bois de Boulogne, the *bucoliques* who work the parks and rural areas, the street girls round Pigalle, Les Halles and the main-line stations, and the teenage girls who frequent the cafés of the Champs-Elysées. Parisian schoolgirls, known as "lollipops", worked these cafés, and also haunted the Porte Dauphine entrance to the Bois de Boulogne, offering fellatio, *la pipe*, at thirty francs a time. At the end of the month, when salaries and allowances ran out, the professionals were supplemented by a wave of amateurs known as *fins-du-mois* or *les étoiles filantes* (shooting stars), comprising "students, secretaries, housewives, poorly paid models – and often daughters of very good families".

The queen of Parisian prostitution, and indeed of the international call-girl market, in recent years was the now-retired Madame Claude, who, as Norma Levy records, "has always worked hand in glove with the French government to provide VIP government guests with all the girls they wanted". Mankoff reports that:

> When the operation is functioning smoothly, there is an active file of from one to three hundred girls, including students, models, housewives, dancers, embassy secretaries, and even a couple of lawyers and doctors.

The rest of Europe has repeated the French pattern, with, of course, local

BRASSAÏ: *Washing in a brothel, rue Quincampoix, c. 1932*

variations, such as the frenetic night-life in pre-war Berlin, so brilliantly captured by George Grosz and Christopher Isherwood. The *Erotic Diary* of the playright Franz Wedekind gives us a rare glimpse into the life of a young man-about-town in Wilhelmine Germany and *belle époque* Paris which can stand for all. In 1887 he rejoices that, "If all the tarts in Munich aren't good-looking, then at least all the pretty girls are tarts."

The street life of the Reeperbahn and Herbertstrasse in Hamburg, and the red-light district of Amsterdam, have become established tourist attractions,

PABLO PICASSO: *Les Demoiselles d'Avignon, 1907*

while the German experiment of state-run "Eros Centres", to which I shall return later, has been the most innovative, if regressive, move by any European government to deal with prostitution in recent years.

Throughout Europe, prostitution has remained a significant part of social life, and of the black economy. And for girls throughout Europe, there has been one constant truth, summed up by Jeanne Cordelier:

> Dear Lord in Heaven, I may not be able to see into my own life clearly, but as far as my eye can see there are men brandishing their own bit of insecurity. There's such a long line of them I'll never get to the end of it.

5 RUINED MAIDS

THE STRUCTURES OF PROSTITUTION

In 1866 Thomas Hardy wrote a poem, "The Ruined Maid", about a raw country girl who goes to London, and there encounters her sister, or possibly childhood friend, Amelia. She greets her:

> "O 'Melia, this does everything crown!
> Who could have supposed I should meet you in Town?
> And whence such fair garments, such prosperi-ty?" –
> "O didn't you know I'd been ruined?" said she.

It's a funny poem, and its ironic reversal of contemporary ideas about good and bad girls makes a telling point about the real choices open to the poor. If all prostitutes had Amelia's wit and resilience, and made Amelia's choices for Amelia's reasons, one might simply say, the best of luck to them. But there are other entrances to prostitution than the free choice of a high-spirited girl, and through some of them come maids who are ruined in a less amusing sense.

As ex-prostitute Gloria Lovatt has put it, "it doesn't always take a special sort of girl to walk the streets, just a special sort of childhood." Many studies of prostitutes have suggested a link with sexual abuse in childhood: Gloria Lovatt was raped in a children's home. In one study of teenage street prostitutes, 31% had suffered incestuous abuse. In Jennifer James's study *Entrance into Juvenile Prostitution*, 65% of adolescent prostitutes report a "forced/bad sexual experience" (defined as intercourse), most before the age of fifteen, 23% with fathers, 15% with other relatives, 15% with strangers and 23% with more than one man at the same time.

Gail Sheehy identified four factors in the backgrounds of New York prostitutes: parents who were absent or inoperative (D. Kelly Weisberg reports that two-thirds of teenage prostitutes come from broken homes), an early and brutal sexual experience (often incest), an early teenage pregnancy, and negative attitudes towards men. On the other hand, Perkins and Bennett say that these do not hold true for the Australian prostitutes they studied, and they quote E. Chesser's opinion that "what channels a girl into prostitution is probably the social conditions she encounters when she leaves the family".

I think it is fairly clear that teenage entry into prostitution, from the age of twelve to eighteen, is a different matter from adult entry, and also that sexual abuse and parental neglect are two powerful factors in the backgrounds of many girls who end up on the street. It may be that among a group of teenage girls struggling to survive in a hostile environment, those with histories of abuse will be psychologically predisposed to become prostitutes, perhaps because their feeling of self-worth has already been fatally undermined. It may be that many of those whom Victorian studies termed "feeble-minded" fell into this category.

Another implication of the term "feeble-minded" was that the girls so categorised were strongly sexually motivated, at a time when women's sexuality was suppressed and denied. As well as those who turn to prostitution in their teenage years out of destitution and despair, there are many who drift into it through sexual precocity. Phebe Phillips, who published her memoirs *Woman of the Town* in 1809, writes that from the age of fourteen she was "tortured . . . by appetite". Her father was a respectable tradesman in the City of London and her mother was a clergyman's daughter, and her parents, noting warning signs, tried to frighten her with horror stories:

> Then I heard most melancholy and dismal accounts (which my father, being church-warden, made to be oftener talked of) how wretchedly a poor street-walker died in the street, or was sent to Bridewell half naked; and these events always concluded with one observation, that all females of that class must come to the same end.
>
> Shocked at these relations, I used to retire often to my chamber, and cry; vow I never would be abandoned, never be a strumpet; and yet in ten minutes a sudden glow of desire filled my mind, and I was all frantic for possession; especially when I observed women, whom both my father and mother knew to be prostitutes, to stop at our door in their own equipages. When I saw the respect that was paid them, I supposed the terrible stories I had heard were only invented to frighten me. I therefore determined to be as gay and as happy as the most famous woman of pleasure upon the town.

After the teenage years, the decision to become a prostitute is more likely to be a freely made choice, of the type described by Lee, a thirty-seven-year-old prostitute running two houses in Sydney, to Roberta Perkins:

ANONYMOUS PHOTOGRAPH: *Lou Bunch, brothel madam, 19th century*

I began when I was nineteen and met some working ladies. I was intrigued by what they were doing and saw the money they had and what they could do with it. I used to sit there and just pick their brains. They didn't encourage me in any way; I just thought: "Well that's one way of making money and getting what I want out of life."

Entry to the profession in adult life is more likely to be controlled by the prostitute herself. Many women who choose to work as prostitutes in their twenties or thirties may work as call-girls, either independently or via an escort agency, or as nightclub hostesses, or as masseuses, or in some form of brothel, while for teenage prostitutes the harsher world of the streets is the only alternative.

Within prostitution there is both a very real sense of shared experience and common cause and a distinct hierarchy of status, with streetwalkers at the bottom. As John M. Murtagh and Sara Harris put it, "Call-girls, house-girls, and night-club prostitutes regard streetwalkers as the lowest women in their business and in the world."

On the other hand the streetwalkers themselves may feel, like B., that "Being on the street is being a real prostitute" (Jaget, *Prostitutes: Our Life*). She compares the street and a brothel to "a fairground and a boarding school"; ordinary women can work in brothels "for the fun of it" but on the street you're "put on file" by the police. The mutual incomprehension of the two worlds of call-girl and street prostitute are well shown in a comic interlude in Sydney Biddle Barrows' *Mayflower Madam*, as Sydney, owner of the most exclusive escort agency in New York, is carted off to court with a round-up of girls off the street:

"What are you in for?"
"Promoting prostitution."
"First time?"
"Yes."
"Don't worry, honey, you'll be out in no time."
"That's good."
"What are all those newspaper dudes doing here?"
"I ran an escort service, and they think it's a big deal."
"You mean you ran some kind of *house?*"
"Sort of." I tried to explain that we were an outcall service, but none of them understood what that was. Finally, I told them I was a madam.
"What?"
Out of the dark came a voice. "That's a female pimp, fool!"

ERNST LUDWIG KIRCHNER: *Street with Red Cocotte, 1914-1925*

The girls who worked for Sydney Biddle Barrows' Cachet were attractive, well-educated, middle-class women, able to hold their own in a social setting with businessmen and diplomats. They were as far from the spandex-clad Manhattan streetwalker as could be, and yet the street girls responded to her with camaraderie rather than scorn or envy, cheering her exit to the courtroom with a good-natured, "Go get 'em, girlfren'!"

The hierarchy of prostitution is also a ladder which can be climbed or descended. Roberta Perkins interviewed Bonnie who, at thirty-three, was now an addicted street prostitute but had been "a high-class, globetrotting hooker". On the other hand it is common for girls who gain experience on the street to move upmarket, like Lynn Keefe, author of *How did a Nice Girl Like You Get Into This Business?*, who became a prostitute in her late teens, after a promiscuous adolescence culminating in an illegitmate baby at eighteen. She writes:

> In 1955 I was at Charleston, South Carolina, working what we girls in the business call the "assembly-line". The only tarts who work the line are has-beens who can't make it in the first-class markets any more or young chicks trying to pick up experience, technique and finesse. I was in the second category. I was able to quit the business before age, circumstance, or both, forced me into the first category. The assembly line is the very bottom of the hooker's social totem pole.

In Charleston, a navy town, the price of a trick was $10 on payday, dropping to $2 as the men ran out of money. Lynn Keefe went on to become a call-girl in Miami, and remained at the top of her profession for ten years, when she retired. She writes of her progression from worker on the assembly-line to call-girl that, "I found that the more money there was involved in a trick, the less important my role as a sex partner, and the more important my role as a companion became."

Even on the street there are patterns of status and seniority, reflected in the claiming of the best positions by the older and more experienced women, but also the frequenting of higher socio-economic areas by the younger and most attractive ones. And as Phebe Phillips discovered, when she was reduced to a "common street-walker" after living an easy life as a kept mistress, and receiving "the politest gentlemen of England" in "a private assembly-room", a place on the street has to be earned or paid for:

> The first evening I took my stand in Fleet-Street, to look out for a fare, I was drove from street to street by women of my own profession, who swore I should not come in their *beats* until I had paid my footing.

On the street, questions such as this are also likely to involve the power and influence of pimps, who are in themselves a source of status in the world of street prostitution. The common assumption that all prostitutes have pimps, to whom they are in thrall, is a misapprehension. Although Ben L. Reitman's 1931 study of Chicago pimps is entitled *The Second Oldest Profession*, the exploitative pimp who runs a string of girls, beating them up if they don't make enough money for him, seems to be a relatively recent development. The word pimp was originally interchangeable with pander or procurer, and in the nineteenth century, when the modern pimp began to emerge, he was first known as a "bully" or a "fancy-man".

The fashion for pimping seems to have developed in France, where Parent-Duchatelet noted that the Parisian girls often chose legal or medical students as their pimps, though many were less refined sorts such as Nana's pimp Fontan in Zola's novel. John Binny, writing in 1861, noted that it was the French prostitutes in London's Haymarket who had fancy-men, while "The generality of the girls of the Haymarket have no bullies".

An 1837 description of one London pimp establishes the type. Vampire Tom was "very nearly six feet high; part of his head is eaten away by a certain disease; very attenuated legs; dark hair and eyes, rather a long nose, and very offensive breath."

1837 is also the publication date of one of the earliest fictional descriptions of the relationship between a prostitute and her fancy-man, in Dickens's *Oliver Twist*. Dickens made no bones in his preface that "the girl is a prostitute", but many readers must have missed entirely how Nancy makes her living. Indeed she is not very realistically portrayed, except in this crucial instance of her dependence on Bill Sikes in an intense relationship based equally on love and fear. She tells Rose Maylie, "I am drawn back to him through every suffering and ill-usage; and I should be, I believe, if I knew that I was to die by his hand at last." Nancy's devotion to the brutal Sikes was denounced as unnatural by readers, but Dickens responded:

> It is useless to discuss whether the conduct and character of the girl seems natural or unnatural, probable or improbable, right or wrong. IT IS TRUE. Every man who has watched these melancholy shades of life, must know it to be so.

The relationship between prostitute and pimp is a complex one. In some ways it is a reversal of society's accepted order, with the woman going out to work in order to keep the man in a life of ease, and it may be that part of the attraction for some women is the feeling of working for someone else. It may be a help through unpleasant moments to know that one is not working for oneself but for one's partner; certainly a similar motive has sustained many men in boring or disagreeable jobs. The main dynamic of the relationship, at least from the woman's side, is simple enough: everyone wants someone to love. And while many prostitutes have boyfriends or husbands who are not pimps (though they run the same risk of prosecution for living off immoral earnings), the particular relationship between pimp and whore, sanctioned by the prostitution culture, is an easier one to sustain. It is only in this emotionally-charged relationship that the pimp's standard threat that he will not sleep with his whore if she does not fulfil her quota could have any effect.

While some girls are duped into prostitution by unscrupulous and violent pimps, the relationship is not usually so one-sided. For instance the Toronto cab-driver John Davidson, in his study of Toronto street life, *The Stroll*, is contemptuous of pimps, who treat the girls as slaves, but he also recognises that it is in a sense a willing slavery. Barring a girl's own emotional dependence, he writes, "there's nothing to keep her with a particular pimp, and it is not uncommon for them to change. The hookers call it 'choosing' a pimp; sometimes they cruise round the stroll looking to spot new pimps." George Kneeland's 1913 New York City survey painted a similar picture of a culture in which "prostitutes often select young men whom they see in front of pool rooms and cigar stores and actually invite them to become their pimps and share the proceeds of their business".

"Choosing" a pimp is of course not simply a matter of emotional importance; the pimp has a key role in some street cultures in organising and overseeing the business of prostitution, and there are sound reasons why any woman working in the harsh and vulnerable world of street prostitution might choose a strong and efficient manager. In addition, within the social world of the street prostitutes themselves, status may derive from the pimp, just as for other women status may derive from the husband.

Bernard Cohen, in his 1980 sociological study of prostitution in New York City, *Deviant Street Networks*, makes an important distinction between "pimps" and "men":

> A *pimp* is a professional whose primary occupation is managing prostitutes. His duties include their recruitment, selection, training, and supervision. Although pandering techniques vary, a typical pimp in New York City

LUCIEN METIVET: *A girl and her pimp, 1899*

manages a stable of two to eight girls and lives off their earnings. A pimp also controls the proceeds obtained through prostitution by doling out spending money to each prostitute and many times even paying their rents and other fixed expenses.

A "man" on the other hand works with one rather than several prostitutes:

He may be the prostitute's lover or husband, and he shares the proceeds from prostitution. Or he may simply be a friend or acquaintance of the prostitute and receive monetary payment for his services.

ANONYMOUS PHOTOGRAPH: *A streetwalker in Rome, 1965*

These services are, essentially, "on-the-spot protection and supervision".
Pimps – apart from those Parisian students – seem to arise in under-classes, among those whose entry to more conventional entrepreneurship

is blocked. Pimping in London's Soho in the 1950s was controlled by Maltese immigrants; in the United States it has generally been the province of blacks. Bernard Cohen identified 97 "deviant managers" (pimps and men) on the streets of Manhattan: 72.2% were black, 20.6% were Hispanic, and 7.2% were white. All the pimps were black, and while there were some black "men", the majority were Hispanic. In contrast, "the majority of managed women were white (73%) and most relationships involved a white prostitute and a black manager". Christina and Richard Milner, in their 1972 study *Black Players: The Secret World of Black Pimps*, confirm that a white "ho" is a status symbol for a black pimp, and also that those white men who become pimps succeed only by imitating the blacks. This is a strongly inward-looking culture. Because pimping is despised by the straight world, the pimps must look for their sense of self-worth to admiration and support from their peers. Most of the pimps that the Milners met had read Iceberg Slim's famous autobiography, *Pimp*, and regarded it as the rule book of their trade. Fashion among pimps was so distinctive that the Milners report seeing a sign in a shop window offering "Pimping Socks" in the currently favoured pastel shades.

The racial crosscurrents which have produced the black pimp/white prostitute pattern in US street prostitution are complex. There is certainly the attraction of the forbidden for both sides, and also an enjoyment of the reversal of the usual pattern of power between white and black (which reinforces the elements of role reversal in the male/female relationship). Malcolm X recalled a white prostitute known as Alabama Peach who worked for Sammy the Pimp: "What made a lot of negroes around the bar laugh the hardest was the way she would take three syllables to say 'nigger'. But what she usually was saying was 'Ah jes' lu-uv ni-uh-guhs-.' "

The autobiographies of men such as Malcolm X, as well as jazz musicians such as Charles Mingus and Miles Davis, show how firmly enmeshed pimping has been in black street culture in this century. The Milners even record a pimp folktale which justifies pimping by placing its origins in the Garden of Eden: Adam was "the first trick", "Snake was a pimp".

Ben Reitman, a distinctly unorthodox medical practitioner who went to prison for campaigning for birth control, and who dedicated his study of pimps to his former lover Emma Goldman, was employed by a number of Chicago brothels and was on friendly terms with many pimps. He quotes one prostitute, Pauline, as saying, "I would rather have one-fourth of a good negro pimp than the whole of two white ones." Part of the reason for this seems to lie in the style with which the black pimps carry themselves; as

Reitman noted, "If their hearts are not gold often their teeth are." One pimp, Silky, told Susan Hall and Bob Adelman, "My tools are also very expensive. I'm continually sharpening my cars, my jewelry, and my clothes . . . If I didn't have the jewelry and the cars, I couldn't get the girls I get." As another pimp, Dandy, told them, "If a woman wants to be with you, she's going to be with you. If she ain't, she ain't."

Charles Mingus, recalling his own "sudden plunge to pimpdom", remarks that "Pimps are usually pretty calm people, cool but lively, full of laughs and jokes and some are even intellectuals." Reitman agrees:

> I often see them down at the Art Institute and at exhibitions. They are especially fond of the legitimate drama. At the opening night of Eugene O'Neill's *Hairy Ape* I called the attention of Ashton Stevens, dramatic critic of the Herald Examiner, to the fact that there were twenty-five pimps in the audience, many of them with their girls. A play like *Frankie and Johnny*, or Mae West's *Diamond Lil*, will attract half the pimps and whores in town.

He describes a Hallowe'en Dance at which "there were more than two hundred well-groomed, apparently happy pimps who were dancing and skylarking about, apparently unafraid and unashamed". He asked one of the more thoughtful of his pimp friends, Leo, how he justified his work:

> In answer to the question how do I justify myself as a pimp, I justify myself, first, because I have an easy, comfortable life. I have a car and good eats. Whenever I want a drink I can have it. I am comparatively free from arrest. I read books and magazines and go to shows, and I don't like to think about myself as a pimp. I am not the vicious type, the exploiter. I think if I take good care of Lucille I pay my way through life. I use this as a means to an end, that is, to enjoy life.

Leo was uncomfortable about living off a woman's earnings, but had come to the conclusion that, "Of all the hard work in the world the hardest is making a living out of a woman."

How do pimps get their women? Some choose or are chosen from the pool of working prostitutes, but others prefer to recruit and train inexperienced girls. They may hang around railway stations or other likely venues such as New York's Port Authority in search of teenage runaways, or they may pick up girls at dances and the like in a brief feigned romance. Sammy the Pimp could, according to Malcolm X, "pick out potential prostitutes by watching their expressions in dance halls". In her study of *Female Sexual*

HENRI DE TOULOUSE-LAUTREC: *The Salon in the rue des Moulins, 1894*

Slavery, Kathleen Barry concludes that " 'Conning' a girl or young woman by feigning friendship or love is undoubtedly the easiest and most frequently employed tactic of slave procurers . . . and it is the most effective." One girl testified to the New York Select Crime Committee in 1977 that she had been picked up at a bus stop in Minneapolis and put on the streets in New York:

83

At the time I did it because I really liked him, and it was more or less having someone, you know, and he said, you know, to prove to him that I really love him I had to do this because we needed the money. It was things he said, but I did it because I liked him. He made you feel like you were somebody important.

The chief technique of such pimps has always been to separate the girl from her home and family, and instil a new sense of values. One pimp, Brock, told the Milners his method of "turning out" previously straight girls:

It's a brainwashing process; the whole thing is creativity. When you turn a chick out, you take away every set of values and morality she had previously and create a different environment. You give her different friends.

There is an obvious comparison to what happened to Patty Hearst at the hands of her kidnappers.

Pimping today has changed little from the style which was well established when the Bureau of Social Hygiene conducted its survey into New York prostitution in 1912. Then, wrote George Kneeland:

The cigar store, the pool room, the coffee and cake restaurant, are the favourite resorts of the pimps. Here they come to make the deals for their women, to receive telephone messages from their girls on the street or in vice resorts, to plan "line-ups" when a "young chicken" is about to be broken into the business, and to buy drugs for their girls and themselves.

A "line-up" is what today would be called a gang-bang, designed to rapidly break down the resistance of novices.

Pimping is a young man's life. The average age of the pimps noted by Bernard Cohen in Manhattan was thirty-three; by their late thirties, pimps are being supplanted by younger, handsomer, more streetwise models. For most pimps, whose vast incomes have slipped through their hands on gambling, drink and drugs (in the 1930s, the drug of choice was opium; in the 1970s, cocaine), the future is an uncertain vista of poverty and petty crime; for others, a banked fortune may allow for a comfortable retirement. In some cases, pimps have used their position as a springboard into the world of entertainment or legitimate business.

One who retired with money in the bank was Marc, a Storyville pimp who told Al Rose that, "by the time I was seventeen, I had eight broads turnin' tricks for me. I wasn't sellin' no more papers, because I was makin' about

EDGAR DEGAS: *The Madam's Birthday, c. 1879-80*

three hundred a week clear". He adds laconically, "I'd have to lay each one of 'em once or twice a month." Granting and withholding sexual favours is one of the pimp's main sources of control over the relationship; in many cases this seems to be entwined with a sado-masochistic pattern of beatings and reconciliations.

Ben Reitman wrote in the 1930s that, "Some pimps hold their women by genuine love and devotion, some by lying and bluffing, and others by fear and beating," and the same is no doubt true today. The relationship, especially, where it involves several "co-wives", and especially in its frequent violence, is hard for outsiders to understand, but it seems clear that despite coercion in some cases, Dr Harold Greenwald is right when he claims that, "The chief relationship between the pimp and the call girl seems to be an emotional one." This is true, he notes, even though pimps are often not very ardent lovers: "As a matter of fact, the relationship usually was not one of normal sexual relations, but tended frequently to be limited to oral sex."

The extent to which girls move between pimps, and can reject them altogether, is illustrated in the story of Rose, then aged twenty-four, a "beautiful young Italian girl" who had had two pimps and one husband, an ex-customer, but was now single and independent, working in a Chicago brothel in 1931. Her evidence is also valuable for its detailed itemisation of the income and expenses of such a life, during the Great Depression which had cut previous earnings by as much as two-thirds. She told Ben Reitman:

> I work in a joint where there are eight girls, six of them have pimps. The other girl without a pimp is Bobby. She left hers because he beat her up.
>
> We earn about $95 a week, and seldom take a pinch, but have to run often, and sometimes the joint is closed for days or hours. The keeper of the joint takes off $4 a day for board. This is just for our meals, towels and protection. We don't sleep there. I give $1 tip per week to the maid, and $1 a week to the roper.
>
> My expenses are: room $9 a week; meals $1.25 a day; taxicab $3 per week; beauty shop $2 per week; pair of stockings nearly every day, 7 pair for $7; pair of shoes a month, $7; a dress a month, $10; winter coat, $38; silk apron for the joint, $5; and last two months, teddies $2.25 apiece, and I buy six of them a year; cigarettes $1 a week; $3 a week for doctor and medicine.
>
> I give my mother $10 a week. When I had a pimp he wouldn't let me do it. He wanted all the money for himself. I don't work steady. If I am alone I can help my mother and save $40 a week. I hope to God I never have another pimp.

Brothels vary very much in their organisation and atmosphere. A., interviewed by Claude Jaget, having been a prostitute for twenty-five years, worked at eighteen in a "real slaughterhouse" of a brothel in Morocco where the girls worked a fifteen-hour day seeing over a hundred clients a day at six-minute intervals. It was her opinion that "brothels in all their forms are a terrible thing for us". Allison told Roberta Perkins that she left a brothel in Kalgoorlie, Australia, despite the good money she was making, because essentially,

> It was a well-paid jail. You were just locked up, you had twelve-foot gates and bars on your window, and there you were locked in for the night when you went to bed. What else was there to do but eat, sleep and work, and in the end it just got me down.

OTTO DIX: *Brothel Madam, c. 1923*

Phebe Phillips wrote of her time in a brothel that "if any part of a strumpet's life is more wretched, more pitiable than another, sure it is that."

Yet she in turn became a madam, before she married and retired from the profession. Most madams have previously been successful prostitutes themselves, and have retired from active service into a managerial role, much like professional footballers. The madam is in an ambiguous position in relation to the women who work for her, for she must be their helpmeet and support, and at the same time exploit them for the good of the house. A girl in Bradford workhouse in 1871 told the matron before she died, "The mistress of the brothel was everything to me when in health, but when unwell I was turned out of doors without mercy, and the doctor said that I might have died any moment."

On the other hand, Norma Levy describes the trust which existed between her and the madam Jean Horn for whom she worked as a call-girl: "She is the one who stood between me and my clients. It was she who enabled me to have some kind of privacy."

Numbers of madams have written autobiographies, including such famous figures as Ruth Barnes, Pauline Tabor, Polly Adler, and Sally Stanford of San Francisco, of whom a girl who worked for her recalled, "If your fingernail polish was not just right, she sent you home to brush it up." Many madams, such as "Silver-Tongue Jean" of Detroit, have achieved wide fame within their profession; Jean was the acknowledged mistress at teaching the art of fellatio. While undoubtedly some worked the girls ruthlessly, acts of charity and good nature are recorded of many, and the communities they ran may have been more homelike and supportive than many of their workers had ever experienced elsewhere. Most would probably want to be remembered with the words of the Kansas City madam who told Charles Winick and Paul M. Kinsie, "I never exploited a girl and always gave the customers a break."

6 MORALS AND MAGDALENS

PROSTITUTION AND SOCIETY

In March 1668, the common people of London rioted over the Easter holidays, and attacked the bawdy houses, which were, writes Pepys, "one of the great grievances of the nation". When King Charles II was told this, he made the immortal reply, "Why, why do they go to them, then?" This is sometimes rendered as, "If they don't like the brothels, they needn't go to them."

The king's relaxed attitude to the problems of public order and morality which attend all forms of prostitution has not been shared by many other rulers. Throughout history a great deal of energy has been spent on suppressing, disguising or reforming prostitution and prostitutes. As C., a twenty-eight-year-old French prostitute, told Claude Jaget, "Cops and cash, they're the two poles in the daily life of a prostitute."

Not surprisingly, the "vice" squads of police forces have always been notoriously prone to corruption. As one former brothel proprietor told the campaigning journalist W.T. Stead, "The police are the brothel-keeper's best friend, because they shut their eyes. And the brothel-keepers are the best friends of the police, because they pay them."

One of the problems of policing prostitution is that as prostitutes' clients are drawn from every rank of society, including that of the law-givers and law-enforcers, there is a vested interest in not rocking the boat. Frances Finnegan's study of prostitution in nineteenth-century York, for instance, turned up the interesting statistics that one in six of the clients who can be identified were policemen, a proportion exceeded only by labourers. In October 1849, for instance, P.C. Whitwell was fined a shilling a week for ten weeks for the twin offences of drinking on duty and "having indecent intercourse with prostitute Isabella Ogram in a passage in Castlegate."

Most societies, with periodic periods of licence and repression, opt largely for an "out of sight, out of mind" approach, concentrating on keeping prostitution tidy rather than on eradicating it. Interaction between police and prostitutes becomes, as Bernard Cohen puts it in his study of Manhattan street vice, "a game of hide and seek". The Manhattan vice squad are referred to as the "pussy posse" by officers and prostitutes alike; in London they are the "tom squad". Yasmin, a London prostitute, told Nickie

Roberts that, before her first arrest, "we used to have a laugh on the street; it was actually funny, running away from the law; it was exciting; it was great fun – like being a mischievous child all over again."

Jill Harsin's *Policing Prostitution in Nineteenth-Century Paris* is probably the best and fullest description of the symbiotic relationship which develops between police and prostitutes. Her study covers a crucial period in which, as she writes, "The *fille publique*, once viewed primarily as an outcast, had been redefined as a threat to public health." The French response was to set up a complex system of registration and licensing, and to pursue those who operated outside this system with indiscriminate brutality. The police raids known as *rafles*, in which any woman who got in the way would be arrested without mercy, are brilliantly described in Zola's *Nana*:

> "It's the police! Come on! Come on!"
> There followed a wild stampede through the crowd. Skirts streamed out behind, and dresses were torn. There were blows and shrieks. A woman fell to the ground. The crowd stood laughing and watching the brutal tactics of the police as they rapidly closed in.

Generally speaking, the policing of prostitution is concerned with the punishment of prostitutes rather their protection. Police and court officials are well aware of the futility and nonsense of imposing fines which actually increase prostitution, as prostitutes work ever harder to pay them off, but in many countries, Great Britain and the United States included, that vicious circle is what counts for a policy on prostitution.

It can be argued that prostitution is inextricably linked with petty – and in some cases organised – crime, and that it must inevitably be a focus of strict police attention. Frances Finnegan notes that in the nineteenth century, "there was a submerged class of petty criminals in York, an underworld of disreputable beer- and lodging-house keepers, fences, thieves and thugs who assisted the prostitute in her work." That work, as Finnegan shows, included "rolling" drunken clients and relieving them of their loose cash and valuables. But the criminality of the prostitute is to some extent the result of anti-prostitution laws rather than the cause of them. It is a chicken-and-egg situation.

There is no easy answer to this problem, but it does seem ridiculous that prostitution laws, in criminalising the women who work as prostitutes, should expose them so cruelly to exploitation and customer violence. Even when public opinion has changed, the process of translating that change

VINCENT VAN GOGH: *The Dance Hall at Arles, 1888*

into legislation is frustrating and slow. Two attempts in Britain in recent years to abolish imprisonment for soliciting offences and remove the hated term of "common prostitute", Maureen Colquhoun's "Protection of Prostitutes' Bill" of 1979 and Clive Soley's "Imprisonment of Prostitutes (Abolition) Bill" of 1981 both passed readings in Parliament but failed to become law for procedural reasons.

The way in which prostitution laws operate, victimising women who may already be victims, represents a kind of institutionalised misogyny. As numerous researchers have pointed out, the laws tend to be applied in a manner which is also racist: Bernard Cohen observed in Manhattan that police were more likely to arrest black or Hispanic streetwalkers than white ones.

This misogyny is sometimes overt, as when a Greenwich Village police sergeant told Susan Brownmiller in 1972 that rape complaints represented "Prostitutes who didn't get their money," but it is essentially covert, unrecognised even by those who apply it. It is embodied in the crucial mistakes made in the police hunt for the serial killer of women, Peter Sutcliffe, known as the Yorkshire Ripper.

As Joan Smith brilliantly shows in her essay on the Ripper case in her book *Misogynies*, the police wasted five years "on wild goose chase for a man they visualized as a reincarnation of Jack the Ripper." The police constructed their entire investigation around the theory that the killer was motivated by a hatred of prostitutes, and ignored or twisted all evidence to the contrary. In fact, none of Sutcliffe's first three victims was a prostitute; the third, a fourteen-year-old girl, had actually provided an excellent photofit picture of her assailant. The police attitude is well conveyed in the words of a senior West Yorkshire detective, Jim Hobson, at a press conference in October 1979:

> He has made it clear that he hates prostitutes. Many people do. We, as a police force, will continue to arrest prostitutes. But the Ripper is now killing innocent girls. That indicates your mental state and that you are in urgent need of medical attention. You have made your point. Give yourself up before another innocent woman dies.

At Sutcliffe's trial, the Attorney General remarked that in his view the fact that some of the victims were not prostitutes was "perhaps the saddest part of this case".

Of course police attitudes to prostitution reflect and enforce the will of society as a whole. The *Très Ancien Coutume* of Normandy, written down about 1200, sanctions the rape of prostitutes, a provision which is also frequently found in Germany and Italy in the Middle Ages. Jacques Rossiaud's research into prostitution in medieval Dijon shows that about half of the women were put into prostitution by force, twenty-seven per cent of these being the victims of public gang rapes directed at women who had attracted social disapproval: "One carpenter's wife was raped 'because she is bawdy and laughs a lot' and called to people in the street by their name." These were semi-sanctioned assaults which seem to have had the function of a "rite of passage" to manhood and possibly admission to neighbourhood gangs for the youth of Dijon. Records show that half of the city's young men participated in at least one gang rape of this kind, with no or negligible punishment.

In sixteenth-century French law, the rape of a prostitute was no longer considered a crime, and many prostitutes report from experience that the same is effectively true today. It is felt that a prostitute cannot be raped, rather than that, because of her working conditions, the prostitute is particularly vulnerable to assault and rape.

Not all police "harassment" of prostitutes is ill-intentioned. In her study *The Invisible Children*, Gitta Sereny gives a very interesting account of the work of Sergeant George Trapp, who in 1976 formed the "New York Pimp Squad". Trapp had 1,700 pimps on file, and his energies were directed at providing some help to teenage runaways lured into prostitution. When one girl complained of being arrested too frequently, Trapp explained: "In her case, and with other very young ones too, we deliberately take them in quite often to let their pimps know that we've got our eyes on them. It's the only protection they've got." Mimi Silbert's report on *Sexual Assault on Prostitutes* quotes one fourteen-year-old girl graphically describing why such protection is necessary. She said:

> The movies and television and books make you think it's glamorous. But you don't feel independent and wanted. You feel like a piece of hamburger meat – all chopped up and barely holding together.

A good many teenage prostitutes either turn to drugs to cope with the life, or turn to the life because they have become drug addicts. One German heroin-addicted child prostitute, Christiane F., has produced an autobiography which chillingly describes her sordid and miserable existence adrift in the counter-culture.

Drugs, alcohol and the crimes associated with them have certainly played their part in the history of prostitution. Just as many prostitutes' clients are drunk or high, many prostitutes have felt the need for a little extra something to get them through the night. Bracebridge Hemyng interviewed in a public house one soldiers' prostitute who, he had been told, was very violent:

> "Passionate!" she replied: "I believe yer . . . You see this public; well, I've smashed up this place before now; I've jumped over the bar, because they wouldn't serve me without paying for it when I was hard up, and I've smashed all the tumblers and glass, and set the cocks agoing, and fought like a brick when they tried to turn me out, and it took two peelers to do it; and then I lamed one of the bobbies for life by hitting him on the shin with a

bit of iron – a crow or summet, I forget what it was. How did I come to live this sort of life? Get along with your questions. If you give me any of your cheek, I'll _____ soon serve you the same.

The connection between prostitution and drugs runs deep, as prostitution is almost the only way many drug addicts can supply their needs, but there is a law of diminishing returns at work, for it is very hard for an addict to function effectively. Despite the extra element of control which drugs would give them, most pimps refuse to work with addicts. Most forms of prostitution require an alert mind and a certain degree of physical fitness incompatible with the abuse of hard drugs.

The health of prostitutes has always been a matter of public concern because of the spread of venereal diseases. The 1161 statutes for the London stews specifically outlaw the employment of women "with the perilous infirmity of burning"; in the early fourteenth century, Edward II opened the first Lock Hospitals, one in Southwark for women and one in Kingsland for men.

Pre-twentieth-century treatments for venereal disease were both painful and inefficient, though a man such as Boswell might suffer numerous doses of "the clap" followed by mercury treatments and come out relatively unscathed. Prostitutes' memoirs are usually fairly coy on this point, though Anne Sheldon's late eighteenth-century account does describe one bout of illness, treated by a prostitutes' physician, Dr Chiddick, from which she recovered. She was also treated by Sir Caesar Hawkins, who later treated free of charge a girl whom Ann helped to return home and marry her former suitor. The girl had been on the point of marriage to this "young and wealthy farmer" when she was taken to London by a procuress known as Mrs White. She told Ann:

> The consequence of this journey on which I expected to enjoy so much pleasure, and to acquire such great improvement, was, with the assistance of Mrs White, my being seduced by Lord Deloraine, who supported me about five weeks, and then left me. An accidental acquaintance with Mr Kildare of Kings-Place, made me afterwards a frequenter of his house, from whence I was inveigled by a Mrs Johnston, who kept me for some time at her house, from where I was persuaded by her partner, Mrs Butler, to go to Dublin, where I was told that fortune would instantly take me into her grace and favour; but all I got there was the disease I now bear about me, – and no sooner did the infamous woman, with whom I lived, perceive my situation, than she removed me to one of the lowest brothels in Smock-Alley, and there left me.

GEORGE GROSZ: *Berlin Night-club, 1920s*

It is hard to give figures for infection rates among prostitutes because these, even when available, often seem highly suspect. In 1912, for instance, Katharine Bement Davis, superintendent of the New York State Reformatory for Women at Bedford Hills, claimed that ninety per cent of her inmates

95

were infected with V.D., but it seems unlikely that her tests or definitions would be accepted today.

Syphilis was, of course, as great a scourge in former times as AIDS is today. Baudelaire and Maupassant are but two of its countless victims. Since the sixteenth century, the disease has cut a wide and deadly swathe through society, halted only by Paul Erlich's development in 1909 of his "magic bullet", the arsenic-derivative salvarsan; effective treatment of gonorrhea was only really possible with the discovery of penicillin in 1941. Before the turn of the century, the two diseases were often confused with each other, as well as with other ailments.

Fear of disease was the motive behind many attempts to regulate prostitution, coming to a peak in the early years of this century. During the nineteenth century countries such as Britain, France and the United States instituted programmes of medical examination of prostitutes, which unfortunately, because of primitive hygiene, probably assisted rather than checked the spread of disease. These humiliating and brutally conducted examinations were everywhere regarded with dread and horror; one girl in 1870 said that, "going up for examination was worse than going with twenty men."

The Contagious Diseases Acts of 1864, 1866 and 1869 were introduced in Britain to control the spread of V.D. in the army and navy. Women in garrison towns could be arrested on suspicion, forcibly examined, and if found to be infected sent to Lock Hospitals; men were not examined. The manifest injustice of this system brought forward one of the great campaigners for women's rights, Josephine Butler, who founded the Ladies National Association for the Repeal of the Contagious Diseases Act, and worked tirelessly for the cause.

Josephine Butler's interest in prostitution began in visits to the Bridewell gaol at Brownlow Hill workhouse in Liverpool. Touched by the girls, she began to offer rooms to those released from the Bridewell, and, when this proved impracticable, opened a "House of Rest . . . for dying Magdalenes". At night she suffered terrible dreams about these reclaimed girls:

> I used to cry out for some way of escape for starving women and saw thousands of them being swept up with a broom and hidden like ashes huge grate by political economists and I kept saying O take care they are tenderer than you.

Homes to reclaim prostitutes were not new. The longest-established, the Magdalen Hospital, was founded by Dr William Dodd in 1758, and a Lock

Asylum had been founded in 1787 for girls leaving the Lock Hospital. By the mid-nineteenth century, social work among prostitutes was almost fashionable. It was, for instance, the chief hobby of Gladstone, even when he was prime minister, and his habit of accosting girls in the street and offering to save them is well documented in his diaries. According to Ronald Pearsall, the girls called him "Old Glad-eye"; D.H. Lawrence's version is "Old Daddy Do-nothing".

Not all efforts at salvation were very successful. The former prostitute Maimie Pinzer, whose letters to her mentor Fanny Quincy Howe between 1910 and 1922 form one of the most important documents in the history of prostitution, writes about one well-meaning but misguided rescue worker that, "every girl in the Tenderloin knows her by the name of 'Creeping Jesus' ". The practice of sending girls who were thought to be "going bad" to prison had the opposite effect from that intended, as one turn-of-the-century girl testified:

> I was no bad girl when I got put away in the Home. Now I know everything bad. I lived with the vilest women, the down-and-out kind, who have taught me and lots of other girls more innocent than I, how to solicit the streets.

For most Victorians, prostitutes were irredeemably "fallen", and their career of vice would lead to inevitable degradation, disease and death. Even those who were sympathetic rather than censorious shared this view, revelling in the pathos of Thomas Hood's poem "The Bridge of Sighs", modelled on the attempted suicide of Mary Furley who threw herself and her child into the Thames in March 1844. The child died, and Mary, who survived, was heartlessly prosecuted and sentenced to death, though later reprieved. Dickens, like many middle-class Victorians, was moved by Hood's poem with its plea for pity and understanding, and its imagery of stained purity. He was deeply affected when he heard it sung, saying "My God, how sorrowful and pitiful it is!":

> The bleak wind of March
> Made her tremble and shiver;
> But not the dark arch,
> Or the black flowing river:
> Mad from life's history,
> Glad to death's mystery,
> Swift to be hurl'd –
> Anywhere, anywhere
> Out of the world!

OTTO DIX: *Big City, 1927-8*

The special appeal of this to Dickens is clear; one thinks of his depiction of Martha Endell in *David Copperfield*, and the nightmarish scene in which Little Dorrit and her backward friend Maggy meet the desperate prostitute on London Bridge. Yet while Dickens shares the standard view of the prostitute as "ruined" in his portrayal of Martha in *David Copperfield*, he also offers a way out for Emily in the same novel: emigration.

Emigration was the solution Dickens adopted in one of his most energetically sustained charitable endeavours, the founding and running of the "Home for Homeless Women" in Shepherd's Bush known as Urania Cottage, financed by the philanthropist Angela Burdett-Coutts. Unlike other reformatories for fallen women, such as the Magdalen Hospital, Urania Cottage did not send its inmates back to the streets, but prepared them for emigration to the colonies and either respectable service or marriage in their new countries.

Urania Cottage was one of the best-conceived of all such schemes, but it succeeded only with the pliable and submissive. The more spirited the girls, the more disruptive and unsatisfactory they were. Dickens's letters to Miss Coutts are full of complaints about Jemima Hiscock, who "forced open the door of the little beer-cellar with knives, and drank until she was dead drunk; when she used the most horrible language and made a very repulsive exhibition of herself", or Sesina Bollard, who "would corrupt a Nunnery in a fortnight".

In reality, ruin and emigration were by no means the only options. William Acton, in his *Prostitution*, made it quite clear that prostitutes were not irredeemable social outcasts, but that for many it was "a transitory state" rather than a life's work. Arthur Munby knew a maid-of-all-work called Sarah Tanner who "be independent". She stayed on the game for three years, and then bought herself a coffee-house by Waterloo Bridge and settled down in respectable comfort. It was their independence, and their anger, which the girls had to resign when they entered Urania Cottage.

Acton remarks that many prostitutes in fact made good marriages, as one of Bracebridge Hemyng's interviewees confirmed: "We often do marry, and well too; why shouldn't we, we are pretty, we dress well, we can talk and insinuate ourselves into the hearts of men." Jacques Rossiaud's study of medieval prostitution in Dijon paints a similar picture. Prostitutes tended to retire at thirty. Some entered convents, and others became vagabonds and beggars, but:

> The majority, however, had an excellent chance of finding a new place in society at thirty years of age. They had little to fear from the violence of the young, and were still marriageable. In no way the objects of social rejection and often with contacts among the clergy and men of law, ex-prostitutes could easily find a place as a servant or a wife . . . Marriage was the most frequent end to a career of making a living with her body for women who had roots in the city.

The prostitute has, however, often been treated as an irredeemable outcast by society. Maimie Pinzer writes heartrendingly of the way her family rejected her. She became a prostitute after being abused by her uncle as a child; she lost an eye, possibly through syphilis, and found it very hard to get back on the straight and narrow. Only her extraordinary intelligence and will sufficed, and even then sometimes "I just cannot be moral enough to see where drudgery is better than a life of lazy vice." She writes: "I've got three brothers, a mother and many uncles and aunts and I can't turn to one of them and my brother said he'd consider I'd done the family a kindness if I would get off the earth."

Maimie Pinzer in fact devoted the rest of her life to work among girls at risk in Montreal, establishing in her own loving and selfless manner a pattern of patience and understanding which could serve as a model for modern social workers.

7 TRICK OR TREAT

THE PROSTITUTE AND THE CLIENT

The relationship of the prostitute and her client is one of great complexity. It is a relationship based on control, but who is in charge depends on your point of view. Superficially, the client seems the dominant partner. He has paid for his pleasure, and can expect the woman to indulge any fantasy and comply with any act he may require. But this illusion of mastery is, in fact, simply part of the service he has bought. It is not real. As Margo St. James puts it in her contribution to *Good Girls/Bad Girls*, "In private, the whore has power. She is in charge, setting the terms for the sexual exchange and the financial exchange." Barbara, a Californian prostitute, confirms this: "I like the power that I have with men. I like making them do whatever I want them to do."

Martin O'Brien's travel book *All the Girls* is essentially a customer's eye-view of the world's prostitutes. In all his stories, it is clear that it is the women who are in charge of the what, where and how of the experience. Even when he is offered the extensive "menu" of a brothel such as Nevada's Mustang Ranch, he is guided gently but firmly to the required choice. In fact he revels in this, comparing the girl he calls Polkadot to "a Norland nanny supervising her charge's bath-time", and wondering wistfully "why couldn't it always be like this?"

There is more in O'Brien's comparison than mere wit. The prostitute's client is in many ways more like a wilful child being humoured by a nanny than a masterful potentate enjoying a concubine. It is I think this sense of looking after the childish side of an outwardly mature man which many women enjoy in their clients. For the idea of the man-hating prostitute, while it has some grounding in fact, by no means tells the whole story. As Cathy, a Canadian prostitute, puts it in *Good Girls/Bad Girls*, "I like my clients . . . I think every prostitute, to a certain extent, has cared for some of her clients. They're not bad people."

Clearly this sense of humanity in the relationship between prostitute and client is more likely to surface in some contexts than others. An escort who is wined and dined by a client in a meeting which has the semblance of a normal date is more likely to value him and be valued in return as an individual, than a girl "working the flats" in London who is probably servicing fifty men a day in gruelling twelve-hour shifts. Nevertheless it seems that those who get the most out of prostitution, in every sense, are those who take a professional pride in their ability to "get on" with their clients, and who enjoy the variety of human nature as it is revealed to them.

Elaine, who initiated Dolores French into the profession, told her: "Part of the art of prostitution is using sex to create a feeling of trust and intimacy, to bring people in touch with their own self-worth." Dolores incorporated this insight into her working life from the start, and her book *Working: My Life as a Prostitute* is full of the pleasure she took in pleasing her clients. She writes:

> As I started working, I found out that many of my clients were isolated and lonely. They would read an ad and answer it because they didn't have anyone else. If I could make that client walk out of the door feeling happy, feeling good about himself, feeling he might actually be interesting and fun to be with, I had performed a great service. To do that a person has to love men and enjoy being with them, which I did.

Dolores French enjoys her work and feels a sense of pride and self-respect which allows her to like her clients. Those women who feel degraded and despoiled by working as prostitutes, who are working for pure financial necessity, may well turn their self-loathing onto their clients. Yasmin, a London prostitute, for instance, told Nickie Roberts: "Punters, now. They make me feel sick. They make me feel ill. Imagine having to lie with somebody you don't want to be with, with no feelings whatsoever. Some of them are grotesque; fat – horrible." But Yasmin adds, "I must say the majority treat me like a human being; I *make* them." In fact, she realises, "I don't like them because I don't like doing what I do."

Women working as prostitutes are, of course, peculiarly vulnerable to male violence. Many working women have stories of sexual assault or rape, and their situation is worsened by the attitude of most police forces that "prostitutes can't be raped". Of 121 prostitutes in Australia surveyed by Roberta Perkins and Garry Bennett, 41 claimed to have been raped while working, and 58 to have suffered violence other than rape. But even in less extreme situations, all prostitutes have clients who repel or disgust them. Madeleine, working in the 1880s, had such an encounter with a "beast", "a man whose name was famous in 'big business' and whose beautiful wife was a leader of society". This man had already been busy all night with another girl, Blanche Audley, who passed him on to Madeleine on the grounds that "if she were forced to endure him for another moment she felt that she would kill him". Madeleine had to recruit another girl, Olga, in order to cope with the man's demands. She and Olga made a good deal of money out of him, principally by selling him the same bottle of champagne many times over, but it was "an afternoon of horror". She writes:

> With drunken liberality he gave us money as freely as he had bought wine, but he extracted his pound of flesh for his money. From the time he came into the room at one-thirty until he fell asleep at seven he pawed over us constantly, until every inch of my flesh was in a quivering revolt against his huge, hairy hands and I was strangling a sob at every breath I drew.

For most prostitutes, such experiences are the worst aspect of their work, though Dr Harold Greenwald, in his "social and psychoanalytic study" *The Call Girl*, did perceive a strong element of masochism in the girls he interviewed.

The prostitute cannot exist without the client. Indeed, the economics of the relationship mean that there are inevitably many more clients than prostitutes. The recent survey of prostitution in Birmingham conducted by Hilary Kinnell estimates that Birmingham's 1,000 prostitutes service between 30,000 and 80,000 men, about half from the city itself and half from the surrounding area. But the writings of prostitutes' clients are even scarcer than those of prostitutes. The conjunction of satyriasis and boastfulness which gave us George Simenon's memoirs is rare, and few autobiographies contain any admission that the writer has frequented prostitutes. Diaries, such as those of Pepys and Boswell, are sometimes franker, but unfortunately those men who have unashamedly reported their appetites and activities are often too self-centred to tell us much of interest. The charlatan magician Aleister Crowley, for instance, records in his diary many encounters with prostitutes with whom he performed acts of 'sexual magick', usually buggery, but we learn very little about the girls beyond their names and a brief description. Perhaps this is often the case with prostitutes' clients, that they are too wrapped up in their own private fantasies to care much about the personalities or feelings of the women whom they pay to enact them. Nevertheless there are exceptions.

The most important of these in the nineteenth century is the anonymous sex-addict known as Walter, whose prodigious sexual history *My Secret Life* records not just sexual acts but conversations with many prostitutes.

OTTO DIX: *Couple, 1926*

102

There seems no doubt that Walter's picture of nineteenth-century prostitution is the most trustworthy and detailed we have, and that in it this most assiduous of clients has faithfully set down the words and characters of the women whose company he sought.

One of the problems of relying on such material as *My Secret Life*, or the memoirs of roués such as Casanova or Frank Harris or Henry Miller, is that in recording the experiences of men whom it is currently fashionable to call "sexaholics", they misrepresent the more workaday nature of the regular client. The writer Samuel Butler, for instance, author of *Erewhon* and *The Way of All Flesh*, catered for his bachelor desires with cold-blooded regularity, allowing – one might even say prescribing – himself one session a week with Madame Dumas in Islington, at precisely 2.30 every Wednesday.

The roistering *London Journal* kept by the young James Boswell in 1762 and 1763 is one of the best records we have of the life of a young man-about-town. Boswell keeps making moral resolutions which in moments of ardour he finds impossible to keep. On Thursday 25 November 1762, for instance, although he "determined to have nothing to do with whores":

> I was really unhappy for want of women. I thought it hard to be in such a place without them. I picked up a girl in the Strand; went into a court with intention to enjoy her in armour [a sheath]. But she had none. I toyed with her. She wondered at my size, and said if I ever took a girl's maidenhead, I would make her squeak. I gave her a shilling, and had command enough of myself to go without touching her.

Boswell subsequently took the precaution of purchasing his own washable condom made of treated linen (more expensive ones were available made of sheep-gut). On Thursday 31 March 1763, for instance, he records that:

> At night I strolled into the Park and took the first whore I met, whom I without many words copulated with free from danger, being safely sheathed. She was ugly and lean and her breath smelt of spirits. I never asked her name. When it was done, she slunk off. I had a low opinion of this gross practice and resolved to do it no more.

Boswell in such a mood is the living proof of the old adage that "A hard cock knows no conscience", or, as the courtesan Harriette Wilson more delicately put it, "There's no wisdom below the girdle."

There never seems to have been much problem for prostitutes to find

WILLIAM HOGARTH: *The Rake's Progress, the Orgy, 1735*

clients, although they have over the years advertised their wares in many ingenious ways.

There is perhaps no typical client, but there are groups of men who can be identified as potential clients. Firstly, there are men living a communal life without women, such as soldiers, sailors and migrant workers. Brothels in ports are always busiest when a ship comes in; garrison towns are always centres of prostitution. In wartime, prostitution whether in the form of "camp followers" or field brothels has always been a fact of life. On the Western front in the First World War, for instance, there was a well-organised system of military brothels, identifiable by a blue lantern if they served officers, and a red one if they served the ranks. Robert Graves's *Goodbye to All That* has a vivid account of one such establishment:

> The Red Lamp, the army brothel, was around the corner in the main street. I had seen a queue of a hundred and fifty men waiting outside the door, each to have his short turn with one of the three women in the house. My servant,

who had stood in the queue, told me that the charge was ten francs a man – about eight shillings at that time. Each woman served nearly a battalion of men every week for as long as she lasted. According to the assistant provost-marshal, three weeks was the usual limit: "after which she retired on her earnings, pale but proud."

Secondly, there are unmarried young men, such as Boswell, or H.G. Wells, who in his twenties went "furtively and discreetly" to a prostitute to lose his virginity. The minor man of letters Frederick Ryman may stand for many, as he records in his diary in 1885 a visit to Sue Best's brothel in Hudson City, New York. He was twenty-seven at the time:

> I was simply suffering for something and I felt as if I should go crazy if I did not get it soon & I don't know but it is cheaper and more fun to pay a professional than it is to fool around with those d___d nonentities who cackle so much about virtue. This only cost me $2.00 & I had $5.00 worth of fun I can swear.

Thirdly, there are married men. The wife may be ill or pregnant, or simply less keen on sex than the husband, or the husband may have desires he feels unable to admit to his wife, but the dominant reason is probably the search for variety, partly in an attempt – even though the woman's acquiescence is purchased – to bolster the man's sexual ego by a new "conquest". Samuel Pepys is typical of many straying husbands when, "in an idle and wanton humour", he walks back and forth past the whores in Fleet Alley, struggling with his conscience.

Fourthly, there are men who feel inadequate or unattractive, or who are impotent.

Fifthly, there are many men whose desires are in some way aberrant, and for whom recourse to a specialist professional offers probably their only chance of sexual gratification of their own particular quirk.

All these categories overlap, and no doubt one could think of others. But a glance at them will show that, apart from the happily married and monogamous, and individuals of firm moral or religious views, pretty well all male heterosexuals can be regarded as potential clients by the prostitute.

According to the Kinsey Report, sixty-nine per cent of white males in the United States had some experience with prostitutes. The later Hite Report on Male Sexuality, although it did not seek comparable statistics, did gather

HENRI DE TOULOUSE-LAUTREC: *Woman at her Toilet, 1896*

together some answers from respondents which one feels are probably typical of many clients, for instance the man who says that, "I feel you pay for sex every time one way or another." Several – chiming from the opposite viewpoint with feminist radicals – give their opinion that, "All wives are prostitutes." One man said: "I feel it is a fair deal paying. Very often I don't have the time to court a woman, etc., in order to get the sex I need. It's beautiful to just call and have sex and get back to business." This cold, deliberate separation of sexual congress from affection, responsibility or obligation, the perception that uninvolved sex is "beautiful", is strikingly unlike the conventional female linkage of sex with general physical affection and emotional commitment. The situation is cut and dried. As Joe, a two-or-three bouts a day market-trader told Iain Scarlet: "You pay an' she plays."

For some men, such a transaction would never satisfy. Mr D., for instance, told Rowntree and Lavers that, "I wouldn't have a prostitute. It's no good unless you both enjoy it." And the railroad worker Lew told Al Rose about his youthful experiences in Storyville: "One thing, though, I was never satisfied. I don't mean that the girls or the district cheated me – but I always had the feeling afterwards that *life* had cheated me."

Many clients seek to echo conventional courtship in their relations with prostitutes. J., an ex-prostitute studying for a doctorate in psychology, told Kate Millett:

> A lot of them wondered – they want to take you out for dinner, want to talk to you; wanted to mimic the behaviour of lovers. Maybe that's what they want. Some of them really want that – to be lovers. They fall in love with you. That's very hard to take. I never liked that. Because that was crossing the boundary – it wasn't business any more. And this was business, it wasn't love.

J.'s career move, from prostitute to psychotherapist, is not such a large step as it may appear. The needs to which prostitutes cater are varied and complex, and they must skilfully negotiate the intricate byways of human desire. As the middle-class prostitute Mrs H. told the Rowntree and Lavers survey of *English Life and Leisure*, "I'm better than a Harley Street specialist for them, and I cost less."

Some of the specialist services requested include bizarre acts of mutilation which suggest a deep sense of self-loathing; occasionally, things go drastically wrong. In one such case in the 1790s, a musician named

ANONYMOUS: *"That girl seems to know you, George!", Regent Street, 1870*

Kotzwarra asked Susanna Hill, a Covent Garden prostitute, "to split his genitals in two". She refused, but agreed to suspend him from a rope. He strangled to death, but Susanna was acquitted of his murder.

John M. Murtagh and Sara Harris remind us that "Most of the men who visit prostitutes would be considered normal"; a very large proportion are married men. They quote an "intelligent, young red-haired call-girl" named Carole Long on her married clients: "It burns them up not to be lords and masters in their own beds, and so they try to make believe they are in ours." It is true that married men will act differently with prostitutes than with their wives; in particular, they will ask prostitutes for services they would be ashamed to ask of their wives. As B., one of the prostitutes who took part in the French National Hookers' Strike in 1975, told Claude Jaget: "Most of them are weirdos in any case. All their funny habits disgust me, they disgust me, everything they ask me to do disgusts me." But nevertheless, "there's money in it".

The most common of all the quirks for which prostitutes cater is sado-masochism. Indeed there are many prostitutes who specialise entirely in this area, and numbers of them spend a great deal of money on setting up torture chambers with special equipment to cater to their clients' tastes. Edward Ward's *London Spy* of 1709 gives an account of such clients, "Flogging-cullies", which holds true today:

> This Unnatural Beast gives Money to those Strumpets which you see, and they down with his Breeches and Scourge his Privities till they have laid his Leachery. He all the time begs their Mercy, like an offender at a Whipping-Post, and beseeches their forbearance; but the more importunate he seems for their favourable usage, the severer Vapulation they are to exercise upon him, till they find by his Beastly Extasie, when to with-hold their Weapons.

A well-known passage in Otway's *Venice Preserv'd* Act III:1, plundered by Zola for *Nana*, gives similar early evidence for the British taste for punishment and humiliation.

Paradoxically, those who want to be punished and degraded are generally men of power and influence. Kelly, an Australian bondage and domination specialist interviewed by Roberta Perkins, told her that her clients were:

> Well, mostly businessmen, middle age upwards. They were all well dressed, you wouldn't pick them in the street, they could be your boss at work. B & D seems to attract that kind of clientele, as though people in authority want that taken away from them.

Besides physical punishment, such clients may want to be treated as slaves and skivvies, and given menial and degrading tasks to do. In her memoirs, the eighteenth-century prostitute Ann Sheldon delineates one such case, of "a person of very gentleman-like behaviour" who wanted nothing so much as to wash dishes. The client was brought to her house by her mantua-maker, who like many dressmakers doubled as a bawd. She recalls:

EDOUARD MANET: *Nana (the courtesan Henriette Hauser), 1877*

ANONYMOUS: *A scene in a sporting house, 19th century*

I went as gently down stairs as my feet could treat; and, looking over the kitchen-door, I saw the good man, disrobed of his clothes and wig, and dressed in a mob cap, a tattered bed-gown, and an old petticoat belonging to the cook, as busy in washing the dishes as if this employment had been the source of his daily bread, – but this was not all; for while he was thus occupied, the mantua-maker on one side, and the cook on the other, were belabouring him with dish-clouts; he continuing to make a thousand excuses for his awkwardness and promising to do the business better on a future occasion . . . When he had completed his drudgery, and had been sufficiently beaten, he desired the two females to skewer him up tight in a blanket, and roll him backwards and forwards upon the carpet, in the parlour, 'till he was lulled to sleep.

Phebe Phillips, a generation later, set herself up with the proceeds of conventional prostitution in a house in the City, the back door of which for convenience and privacy opened into a churchyard. With three girls to assist her, she catered exclusively for such special tastes. Of her customers, "a staid demure set of old impotent gallants", she writes:

> I can hardly forbear spitting at their memories, when I reflect on the old goatish dotards – their vanities – their lusts – their meanness; and, what seems a paradox, their prodigalities; for though they would spare no expense upon the woman who would gratify them in their loathsome desires, yet would they be pleased if they could pay half-a-guinea short in their reckoning.

Of all her customers of this period, her ridicule is fondest, perhaps, in recalling the harmless, childlike man who would pay her five guineas a time, besides showering her with "pretty presents" in order to be allowed to sit for an hour and comb out her long auburn hair. Harriette Wilson's sister Amy had a similarly quirky client, the M.P. Hart Davis, who used to give her £100 to pat her: " 'Aamy! Aamy!' he used to say, drawing down his bushy eyebrows, and patting me thus – 'Aamy! Aamy! does that feel nice?' " Such fetishes seem to derive from experiences in early childhood.

There exists a document purporting to be a price list from the brothel run by Charlotte Hayes in London's Pall Mall in the 1750s; it was known as the "cloister" and all the girls were referred to as "nuns". The list, for "Sunday the 9th January" was printed in *Nocturnal Revels*, 1779, "by a monk of the order of St Francis". Whether it is fact or fiction, it gives a good idea of the range of services which such a brothel might provide:

> A young girl for Alderman Drybones. Nelly Blossom, about 19 years old, who has had no one for four days and who is a virgin . . .   20 guineas
> A girl of 19 years, not older, for Baron Harry Flagellum. Nell Hardy from Bow Street, Bat Flourish from Berners Street, or Miss Birch from Chapel Street . . .   10 guineas
> A beautiful lively girl for Lord Spaan. Black Moll from Hedge Lane, who is very strong . . .   5 guineas
> For Colonel Tearall a gentle woman. Mrs. Mitchell's servant, who has just come from the country and has not yet been out in the world. . . 10 guineas
> For Dr. Frettext, after consultation hours, a young agreeable person, sociable, with a white skin and a soft hand. Polly Nimblewrist from Oxford, or Jenny Speedyhand from Mayfair . . .   2 guineas

HENRI GERVEX: *Rolla, 1879*

Lady Loveit, who has come from the baths at Bath, and who is disappointed in her love affair with Lord Alto, wants to have something better, and to be well served this evening. Capt O'Thunder or Sawney Rawbone . . .

50 guineas

For his Excellency Count Alto, a fashionable woman for an hour only. Mrs. O'Smirk who came from Dunkirk, or Miss Graeful from Paddington . . .

10 guineas

For Lord Pyebald, to play a game of piquet, for *titillatione mammarum* and so on, with no other object. Mrs Tredrille from Chelsea . . .5 guineas

Charlotte Hayes retired from business with a fortune of £20,000; it would be interesting to know how much of this was made from female clients such as "Lady Loveit".

What men want from prostitutes, as evidence such as this from the eighteenth century shows, does not change much over the years, though anecdotal evidence suggests an increase in the present century, alongside the general sexual liberation of society, in requests for services other than straight intercourse. The American Social Health Association has studied customers since the 1930s, and estimates that while in the United States in the 1930s only ten per cent of men asked for anything other than straight sex, by the 1960s nearly nine out of ten customers were requesting oral sex or "half and half". In the years since then, anal sex has risen dramatically in popularity, though since the appearance of AIDS it has probably dropped even more dramatically, being replaced by behaviour which has a larger element of fantasy and a smaller element of physical contact.

It is hard to know how customers regard prostitutes. The British edition of the magazine *Marie Claire* in November 1990 asked three prostitutes to interview their clients about their reasons for paying for sex. Most of the featured clients showed deep emotional and psychological inadequacies, and a self-loathing which manifested itself in violent words and acts and a seeming contempt for their partners, shared equally between the prostitutes and their wives. Others exhibited a surprising tenderness. It seems as if men's behaviour to, and opinion of, prostitutes, is closely linked to their general attitude to women, especially their wives or girlfriends. As one man told the Hite Report, in a sentence ripe with ambiguities, "I've had sex with prostitutes and found them very much like other women."

8 GOOD GIRLS GO TO HEAVEN, BAD GIRLS GO EVERYWHERE

PROSTITUTION AND SEXUAL POLITICS

The sexual politics of prostitution take us to the heart of the relationship between the sexes. They obviously vary at different levels of society, between different societies, and in different historical periods, but much remains true throughout all patriarchal societies.

The question which this chapter sets out to explore is whether the prostitute must be, as John Wilmot, Earl of Rochester, phrased it, "a passive pot for fools to spend in", or whether she can define for herself a role with more dignity and freedom than this. The Marquis de Sade envisaged an ideal society in which all women were prostitutes, but in that society he also detected a new kind of freedom, exhorting women:

> Charming sex, you will be free: just as men do, you shall enjoy the pleasures that Nature makes your duty, do not withhold yourselves from one. Must the more divine half of mankind be kept in chains by the others? Ah, break those bonds: nature wills it.

Another Frenchman, Charles Baudelaire, wrote in his private journal, "Love is the desire to prostitute oneself. There is, indeed, no exalted pleasure which cannot be related to prostitution." It seems worth pondering for a while what such a statement might mean.

The key to such a reverie might be a comparison of prostitution and marriage, for through much of our history prostitution, marriage and the religious life have been the three clearest choices facing most women. Emma Goldman pointed out early in this century that, "To the moralists, prostitution does not consist so much in the fact that the woman sells her body, but rather that she sells it out of wedlock." But to her, "It is merely a situation of degree whether she sells herself to one man, in one marriage, or to many men."

This concept of marriage as simply a sort of restricted prostitution has been further explored by Angela Carter, in her study *The Sadeian Woman*:

The marriage bed is a particularly delusive refuge from the world because all wives of necessity fuck by contract. Prostitutes are at least decently paid on the nail and boast fewer illusions about a hireling status that has no veneer of social acceptability, but their services are suffering a decline in demand now that other women have invaded their territory in their own search for a newly acknowledged sexual pleasure. In this period, promiscuous abandon may seem the only type of free exchange.

Angela Carter here might echo, with Sade, another of Rochester's insights: "there's something generous in mere lust".

A definition of marriage as prostitution is obviously far too simplistic a view of the most complex social and personal relationship which human society has evolved, but at the cutting edge of the sex war, it has its uses. It enables us to understand, for instance, the anger and frustration of Derek, a regular client of a prostitute named Sheena, whom he visits with his friend Jimmy. When she interviewed him for the magazine *Marie Claire*, he told her:

I don't have to put up with any rubbish from you like I do with my wife – she always wants me to get her in the mood first, and she talks too much. If I'd known marriage was going to be like this I'd never have bothered to stick with one woman in the first place. What the hell's the point in giving her money if I can't get sex on tap when I want?

It is a short step from such an attitude to behaviour such as that of the magician MacGregor Mathers, an associate of the poet Yeats, who forced his beautiful and sensitive wife Moira, the sister of the philosopher Henri Bergson, to become a streetwalker, driving her to a nervous breakdown.

Many men explicitly compare the business of courtship with prostitution. Questioned for the 1951 survey of *English Life and Leisure*, Mr P., a labourer, said that "he can have all the women he wants without having to keep them for the rest of his life". Mr J. concluded that, "If you pay a prostitute there are no complications. And if you take presents and things into account, a prostitute is cheaper in the long run."

The "dating" system as it has developed in Western society has remarkable parallels with monetary prostitution, leading one contributor to the volume *Sex Work*, Donna Maria Niles, to write that, "Any woman who has ever been on a date, who knows what it is to exchange affections or sex for dinner, or kindness, or survival, is quite prepared to be a hooker." The ex-prostitute J. told Kate Millett, "I would so much rather turn a trick with somebody than go out on a date."

Exceptional circumstances will expose these ambiguities in male-female relationships with raw cruelty. One of these circumstances is war, with its accompanying hunger and devastation. In Naples in 1944, the Bureau of Psychological Warfare stated that one-third of the female population of 150,000 was engaged in prostitution, in return for the money, food and goods available to occupying soldiers but not to the Neapolitan men. Norman Lewis, who was stationed in Naples with the Field Security Service, watched this speedy and complete corruption of a society's moral code: "Thus the long, delicate, intricate business of the old Neapolitan courtship – as complex as the mating ritual of exotic birds – is replaced by a brutal, wordless approach, and a crude act of purchase."

An interesting light is thrown on this question of prostitution as a more honest mirror of matrimony in the memoirs of eighteenth-century prosti-tutes. Ann Sheldon, for instance, married for reasons of convenience a midshipman named Archer, only to discover that on her wedding night her husband forbade her to go out, "and talked of his rights as my lord and master; but, to let him discover the opinion which I entertained of them, I quietly left the house, and went to Thornton's Bagnio, in the Piazzas in Covent-Garden." Harriette Wilson firmly told her lover Fred Lamb, when leaving him for the Marquis of Lorne, that "I will be the mere instrument of no man. He must make a friend and companion of me, or he will lose me." As Lamb's wife, she could not have uttered such a sentence.

Margaret Coghlan, an American whose father Major Moncrieffe fought for the British in the War of Independence, was married off by her father to Mr John Coghlan on 28 February 1777, by special licence. She writes:

> At this period, I was only fourteen years and a few months old; so early did I fall a melancholy victim to the hasty decision of well meaning, but alas! most mistaken relations. My union with Mr Coghlan I never considered in any other light, than an honourable prostitution, as I really *hated* the man whom they had compelled me to marry.

Coghlan took her to Britain, whereupon she left him, and threw herself on the protection of one of her father's old friends, Lord Clinton, who "meanly proposed to surrender me, young and beautiful as I was then considered . . . to the arms of one of his libertine companions." As she rejected that

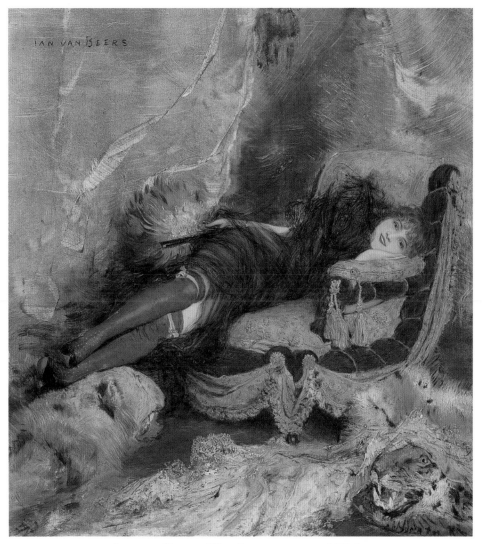

JAN VAN BEERS: *The Courtesan, c. 1890s*

option, it was felt the only course open was "for me to retire to a convent in France". She agreed, but left the convent before long, finding it insufferably boring, and took lodgings with a respectable family near Grosvenor Square. Her father wrote to her that he no longer considered her his daughter, and "advised me to endeavour to learn the mantua-making business", which was tantamount to telling her to become a prostitute. She became the mistress of Charles James Fox, and subsequently a series of gentlemen, enjoying with some of them "all the comforts and delights of domestic life", and bearing children to several of them, including Fox. She fell into debt and moved to Paris, where she lived in a brothel, and was arrested and imprisoned for debt. Released because she was pregnant, she returned to England, where she spent two years in the King's Bench debtor's prison.

Another memoirist, Teresia Constantia Phillips, later Mrs Muilman, has some very interesting things to say in her open letter to Lord Chesterfield. She started out in the world, she writes, "with nothing but my Beauty", well aware of "the Disadvantages we labour under from being born Women". In a key passage, she tells him:

> You will all admit Men may be even profligate in their Amours, and none of you will dispute their being in all other Respects Men of Honour; and, as such, they are admitted into all Companies, and by all Ranks and Degrees of People; And yet, my Lord, this Difference between us has no other Sanction than Custom, cruel unequal Custom!

Phebe Phillips is even more straightforward:

> If any delicate-minded reader should despise me for being so ready to yield my person merely to gratify my luxury, before they blame me, or any of my sex, for there condescensions, let them look upon mankind, examine how they came by their grandeur, and I shall not be thought to hazard too much in asserting, that the males will be found to be the worst prostitutes.

Prostitution and marriage are not, of course, two separate alternatives. Many prostitutes are married. In nineteenth-century New York, for instance, about a third of all recorded prostitutes were married, though not necessarily living with their husbands; prostitution could be a way out of an unsatisfactory marriage, as for Margaret Coghlan. Bracebridge Hemyng writes about married prostitutes in London in 1861:

> A Frenchwoman in the habit of frequenting a notorious house in James Street, Haymarket, said that she came to town four or five times in the week for the purpose of obtaining money by the prostitution of her body. She loved her husband, but he was unable to find any respectable employment, and were she not to supply him with the necessary funds for their household expenditure they would sink into a state of destitution, and anything, she added, with simplicity, was better than that. Of course her husband connived at what she did. He came to fetch her home every evening about ten o'clock.

Furthermore, as we have seen, the majority of prostitutes work between the ages of eighteen and twenty-five, and have retired from the profession by the age of thirty. For many of these women, marriage is the end of prostitution; as Hemyng put it, "a majority of them, eventually become comparatively respectable, and merge into the ocean of propriety".

Phebe Phillips, for instance, retired when she fell in love. She writes about this marriage:

> I doted upon him; my whole delight was in him; I was the girl of his affection; he was the man of my heart. He married a prostitute, one whom he knew to be so; yet he tenderly loved me; my gratitude to him therefore was unbounded.

Unfortunately, the marriage failed. Her husband deceived her and kept a mistress, for whom he left her, whereupon, like Fanny Hill, "I once more retired to my Devonshire estate, where I now employ myself in works of charity." Her reaction to her husband's infidelity strikes a chord with the French prostitute A., interviewed by Claude Jaget, who told him, "I think we've got even more old-fashioned ideas about couples than other people have."

Allan Mankoff notes of the girls in Amsterdam's notorious red-light district that, "Most girls leave the canals by age thirty, may marry, settle to comfortable bourgeois lives." It is from a different section of the community that Jan Bik recruited his Dutch network of "housewife whores", the nearest prostitution has come to domesticating itself and shrugging off its legacy of illegality and squalor. A comparison may be made with the French practice, also described by Mankoff, of "prostitution with basket", in which house-wives go with men who approach them in supermarkets offering to buy their groceries. The fact that the payment is a gift of goods rather than money gives such dealings a veneer of respectability beyond a straight cash transaction.

For those who take the plunge into prostitution proper, though, what benefits can there be, to outweigh the conventional dream of home and marriage? Nadia Miller, who was turned out as a prostitute by her husband within a month of marriage, told Jeremy Sandford: "Basically, I'm glad it's gone the way it has instead of some dreary marriage. Being a prostitute has done a lot for me. I've become a woman through prostitution." Similarly Yasmin, talking to Nickie Roberts, while recognising the downside of the job, and especially its "mental stress", says, "I have no regrets about my life at all; it's made me a woman of the world."

The components of feelings like these, which are expressed by many prostitutes, seem to be, in fairly equal measure, freedom, independence, and power. By freedom I mean the sense of living for the moment, taking life as it comes without responsibilities, which leads John Davidson to say that, "pimps and hookers tend to live like the proverbially irresponsible heirs to an immense fortune." There is a lure in such a life for someone like Teresia Constantia Phillips, who tells us, "I was born constitutionally with the greatest Share of Vivacity and Spirits of any Woman in the World", or twenty-two-year-old prostitute, Miss R., who told the *English Life and Leisure* survey that she wanted: "A short life and a happy one. I don't want to grow old. I'm having a wonderful time now. It might last another ten years. I don't care if I die then." Such women are temperamentally suited to the life, like Lisa, who told Roberta Perkins that:

> I only intended to go for six months, but I liked the money. I wasn't starving or anything, I chose to be a prostitute; maybe I was meant to be one for I've made it my career now for nearly twenty years. I could have got a straight job then, but I preferred to prostitute.

The second attraction of prostitution is its emotional and financial independence, sometimes specifically independence from men. For instance, J. told Kate Millett, "I felt freer of men as a prostitute than I would as a wife or a mistress or a beloved." Kelly, an Australian bondage and domination specialist, told Roberta Perkins of her start in the life working in a massage parlor:

> The first night I worked I did fourteen men, it was all a bit quick for me and I felt disgusting, low and dirty. But I stuck at it for the money. I'd never had so much in my life, and I felt independent. I could buy fancy new clothes and anything I wanted, and I didn't have to go home to my mother.

A Victorian "kept mistress" told Bracebridge Hemyng:

> I am not tired of what I am doing, I rather like it . . . my mother and father don't exactly know where I am or what I am doing, although if they had any penetration they might very well guess. Oh, yes! they know I am alive, for I keep them pleasantly aware of my existence by occasionally sending them money. What do I think will become of me? What an absurd question. I could marry tomorrow if I liked.

GUSTAVE COURBET: *Girls on the Banks of the Seine, 1857*

For some, the idea of being paid for what other women do for free is a pleasure in itself, as in the case of Jan, a beautiful twenty-seven-year-old part-time call-girl, who told Iain Scarlet that she gets "a hell of a kick" out of being paid.

As Marianne puts it in Christina Stead's *House of All Nations*, "There's no subject so rich in ideas as Money." For some people, it seems, the element of purchase in prostitution outweighs in importance the mere physical act. Much of what is really going on between prostitute and client is happening in the imagination.

The third crucial area of job satisfaction is the feeling of power, of being in charge, which prostitution paradoxically brings. Priscilla Alexander reports that, "Many women told me that the first time they felt powerful was the first time they turned a trick." Debra (in Alexander and Delacoste, *Sex Work*) contrasts this feeling with the powerlessness of factory work:

> I've worked in canning factories, which is horrendous work. That's why prostitution was so nice for me. Because you got a lot of money. You didn't take harassment. You didn't allow it. You were in control of the situation. You know?

Zoe, an ex-prostitute and member of the Australian Prostitutes' Collective, described this feeling to Roberta Perkins:

> There is a certain amount of power in straight sex situations because the guys are nervous. They are paying for you, and you can demand what you want and didn't want: no, you can't kiss me, no you can't do that, time's up, whatever. In my personal experience I found it was a total role reversal to the usual men in positions of power and dominance and women subservient to them, and I gained a lot of confidence out of it.

This confidence is partly the confidence to say, with D., one of the French contributors to Jaget, *Prostitutes: Our Life*, "My body belongs to me and I'll do what I like with it." Many prostitutes might echo Karen, who told Harold Greenwald, "Women are afraid of whores because they do what they would like to do themselves . . . Men fear a woman who is bold."

"Bold" women in the past, simply by challenging male notions of female submissiveness, have been assimilated to the ranks of the prostitutes. No clearer example of this can be found than in the theatre. The word actress was synonomous for many respectable people with whore, and indeed in the eighteenth and nineteenth centuries a large proportion of actresses did supplement their meagre wages by prostitution. The price they charged was threefold: freedom, independence, and power.

The historic connection between acting and prostitution was strongly maintained in the United States. In nineteenth-century America as in Europe, no respectable woman would have appeared as actress, singer or dancer on the public stage. Women who appeared as public entertainers in saloons and dance halls, or worked as waitresses in them, were generally also available for sexual hire.

This historical context provides an explanation for the widespread exploitation of would-be actresses in Hollywood, from its beginnings right up to the demise of the studio system in the 1960s, and in varying forms up to the present day. In his light-hearted and anecdotal survey *The Casting Couch: Making it in Hollywood*, Selwyn Ford notes that as early as 1924 an explicit pornographic film starring the teenage Joan Crawford could be entitled "The Casting Couch" with no need for further explanation. The men who ran the film industry seem almost without exception to have demanded and received sexual favours in return for taking an interest in a girl's career. Both starlets and contracted actresses were treated as prostitutes in every way, except that they worked for promises rather than money. Carole Landis was actually known on the lot of Twentieth Century-Fox as "The Studio Hooker", but this explicit connection between film-acting and prostitution rarely seems to have been made. No men and very few women ever seem to have questioned the morality or the sexual politics of the situation, even though the girls, who were mostly used, abused and discarded without ever having had any hope of success in films, were usually inexperienced teenagers. The most demeaning acts, performed either in a producer's office or at the sex parties for which Hollywood was famous, were seen as as "career moves" by the girls and rightful perks by the men. When Marilyn Monroe admitted that she spent most of her early career "on my knees" she was making neither a confession nor an accusation: if anything, she was offering a helpful tip to other young hopefuls on how to get on in Hollywood.

For women like Crawford, Landis and Monroe, the rewards of acquiescence in the system were clear. They achieved riches and fame, if not personal happiness. The rewards for those who did not become stars are less obvious, but while some no doubt felt cheapened and betrayed, many seem to have entered into the party spirit with a swing, buoyed up by hopes that someday their big break would come. For such girls, the excitement of mixing with men of power, who ruled a glamorous dream world quite outside the bounds of everyday life, seems itself to have been an aphrodisiac. One might compare them to the groupies who emerged in the 1960s when the world of pop overtook that of films as the centre of teenage fantasy. Parties held by rock groups had all the Roman orgy characteristics of the standard Hollywood bash, and dressing-rooms were besieged by girls who felt honoured to be allowed the privilege of servicing their hero.

Pamela des Barres, who was a member of Frank Zappa's all-girl rock group the GTO's, has written a refreshingly witty and intelligent account of her years as a groupie, *I'm with the Band*. Describing her teenage years, she writes:

I showed my affection for the opposite sex in those days by giving them head, and I was very popular indeed. I tried not to think of myself as being cheap or easy or any of those other terms that were used to described loose, free, peace-loving girls; I just wanted to show my appreciation for their music, for their taste in clothes, for their heads, hands and hearts. I found myself in many broom closets and backseats with my head buried in many pairs of satin trousers, but I held on to my virginity like it contained the secrets of Tutankhamen.

There was no commercial element in her relations with pop stars, many of whom became friends as well as lovers.

Like the movie starlets of their mothers' and grandmothers' generations, groupies have felt honoured and excited to make themselves sexually available in this way, in the groupies' case without even any thought of reward beyond the pleasure of the act itself. Although this may be connected with the general loosening of sexual behaviour over the same period, it still seems a special phenomenon worthy of proper analysis. It may just be that the modern media have intensified the erotic aura which has always surrounded famous men to such a pitch that even minor film and pop stars now have the kind of magnetic attraction reserved in the past for kings and emperors. Politicians, too, share this aura, as a glance at the life of John F. Kennedy or Mussolini discloses. For an "ordinary" person to share an experience with such a personality is to invest their own lives with a borrowed magic. The encounter may seem tawdry and sordid to an outside eye, but not to the participants.

As the quotation above from Pamela des Barres suggests, even in a libertine age there is still a value to virginity. In the nineteenth century this was so high that a virgin who was seduced or even raped lost her "character" and was virtually condemned to be a prostitute. The Victorian novelist Dinah Mulock was considered daring when she argued in *A Woman's Thoughts Upon Women* that "the loss of personal chastity does not indicate total corruption, or entail permanent degradation".

One consequence of the high regard set on virginity was a high price for it in the prostitution market: so high, indeed, that the artificial restoration of virginity was a thriving trade throughout the eighteenth and nineteenth centuries. The famous bawd Charlotte Hayes claimed that a girl could lose her virginity five hundred times and still pass as a virgin. The nineteenth century saw the growth of what has been termed "defloration mania" in England, and a trade in virgins which was exposed, in lurid and exaggerated but essentially truthful terms, by the journalist W.T. Stead in the *Pall Mall*

JULES PASCIN: *Claudine Resting, 1923*

Gazette in 1885. Stead went so far as to purchase and authenticate a virgin, thirteen-year-old Eliza Armstrong, to prove it could be done, an indiscreet act of investigative journalism which put him in prison.

Stead's other focus of attention beside the rape of virgins in English brothels such as Anna Rosenberg's house in Liverpool, was the trade in English girls sent out from London to brothels in Holland, Belgium and France, for which he could rely on the evidence gathered by Josephine Butler. This White Slave Trade undoubtedly existed, and though it is likely that many of the girls were already prostitutes, or understood that they were to become so, the men and women engaged in the trade were not so delicate of mind as let the girls' willingness or otherwise get in the way of business. A letter exists from the Dutchman Klyberg who throughout the 1870s was, with his wife, the principal importer of girls from London to continental brothels:

> My dear Quoilin,
> You will find me in London early on Tuesday, when you come to fetch your wares. You can take these away the same evening. Everything will be in readiness, and I can guarantee that if you fetch them from London it will only cost you the half of what it would in your own house. I have a lovely tall brunette girl, with glorious teeth, faultless bust; in a word, a beautiful woman, and a good girl. My wife has had her for three weeks, and therefore wrote you. I have also a tall blonde girl when you have room. I am sorry I cannot go over, but I have business in Holland. I have been offered a house in Leyden, and should like to talk to you about it. Sarah, the woman who has the house in Amsterdam, has asked me about two lots, and the people in two other houses are also requiring goods, so that as soon as I can travel I shall make some money, and when I take over the house in Leyden I shall be my own agent and travel continuously. I shall have a lodging in London, where I can come to fetch girls.

The market in flesh which this letter so chillingly evokes still exists, according to modern writers. Kathleen Barry, in her ground-breaking study *Female Sexual Slavery*, describes the small prostitution hotels in the North African quarter of Paris near the Barbès-Rochechouart metro, known as *maisons d'abattage*, literally, slaughterhouses. Here, "six or seven girls each serve 80 to 120 customers a night. On holidays the quota might go up to 150." The girls are kept in debt to the house. According to Barry, "the women may be purchased, kidnapped, drawn in through syndicates or organised crime, or fraudulently recruited by fronting agencies . . . or they may be procured through seduction." She describes a slave trade in European girls destined for Arab harems as still active in Zanzibar in the 1960s.

The precise truth of white-slavery claims has always been difficult to establish because the waters have been so muddied by writers like Stead, but there is no doubt of the central point that by no means all prostitutes chose to become prostitutes or wish to remain so. Kathleen Barry regards all prostitutes as being essentially sexual slaves.

Certainly the idea of forced prostitution brings home very strongly the truth that in prostitution it is almost always males who buy and females who sell. Leaving male homosexual and transsexual prostitutes aside, one can see that whole structure of prostitution as we know it, from the most miserable sex slave to the proudest call-girl, is a creation of the imbalance in power – meaning authority, financial opportunity, independence of action – in the relationship between the sexes.

The literature of prostitution contains scattered references to brothels employing men to service rich women, but there is little reliable evidence that such prostitution ever existed except on the most minor scale. Usually one can detect in such accounts some of the wishful thinking which informed Mary Wilson's plans for a brothel for women, which she called the Eleusinian Institute. Mary Wilson kept conventional brothels in Old Bond Street and other locations in London, and was also a key figure in translating and publishing erotica in the early nineteenth century. She described her Eleusinian Institute in her *Voluptuarian Cabinet* of 1824:

> Any lady of rank and means may subscribe to this Institute, to which she shall always have the entry incognito; the married to commit what the world calls adultery, the unmarried to obey the commands of all-powerful nature, and to offer a sacrifice to the oldest of the gods, Priapus. I have bought a very convenient piece of land, lying between two main streets, from both of which it can be reached through shops in which only women's goods are sold. In this space, between two rows of houses, I have created a very elegant temple, in the centre of which are large salons, surrounded by charming and comfortable boudoirs. In these salons, arranged according to their class, can be seen the most attractive men of all types that I can obtain, expert in all forms of pleasure to suit all tastes, and all in a state of great exaltation produced by good living and inertia. The ladies never enter the salons, but are shown the occupants through darkened windows in the boudoirs. In one room can be seen beautiful, elegantly dressed young men playing cards or music, in others, athletically built males, completely naked, wrestling or bathing. In short, there are so many kinds of these animals for

R.B. KITAJ: *Femme du Peuple I, 1974*

them to look at that they cannot tell which to choose. As soon as their minds are made up, they ring for the chambermaid, call her to the window and show her the object of their desire, and he is forthwith brought to the boudoir.

While many Parisian brothels in the nineteenth century offered services to lesbian clients as well as to men (and of course many prostitutes, especially in the closed world of brothels, have themselves been lesbian or bisexual), it seems doubtful whether any such organisation as the Eleusinian Institute has ever existed. Non-prostitute women have always been able to prostitute themselves in brothels and houses of assignation, and there have always been some men whose activities might qualify them as male courtesans or gigolos, but a brothel full of heterosexual males "in a state of great exaltation" is a fantasy that even the twentieth century has not brought to fruition.

The belief that prostitution always brings its practitioners to a bad end, and that the life of the prostitute is one of unalloyed misery and degradation, is very deeply engrained. In countering it, it would be foolish to suggest that the opposite is true, and that all prostitutes live happy, fulfilled lives of proud independence. The truth is that it is a way of life like any other, with its compensations and drawbacks. Listen to the testimony of Old Stock, a woman of fifty employed as a maid in a Victorian brothel, and also to follow a young "dress-lodger" in the streets to make sure she does not abscond with the valuable clothes, waste time in drinking, or work for a rival house:

> They do say I'm a bit cracky, but that's all my eye. I'm a drunken old bitch, if you like, but nothing worser than that. I was once the swellest woman about town, but I'm come down awful. And yet it ain't awful. I sometimes tries to think it is, but can't make it so. If I did think it awful I shouldn't be here now; I couldn't stand it. But the fact is life's sweet, and I don't care how you live. It's as sweet to the whore, as it is the hempress, and mebbe it's as sweet to me as it is to you.

As she put it, "Ah! gay women see strange changes; wonderful ups and downs, I can tell you."

9 WHEN WHORES START TELLING THE TRUTH

PROSTITUTION TODAY

Feminism and prostitution have had an uncomfortable relationship. For Susan Brownmiller, for instance, in her pioneering study of rape, *Against Our Will*, "The case against pornography and the case against toleration of prostitution are central to the fight against rape." Jess Wells argues similarly that, "prostitution and rape come from the same sexist view of women". The apparent rejection of prostitutes by feminist theorists gave rise to considerable anger at conferences in the 1980s where prostitutes and feminists came face to face, an anger which was voiced to Eileen McLeod by a girl named Julie: "These women's libbers who say we're sex objects – I'm just using my brain as far as I'm concerned. I just wanted to earn a lot of money every week and this is how it happened."

In May 1983, feminists marched through London's Soho vice district to "Reclaim the Night". Nickie Roberts, who was working there as a stripper, recalls, "The only women who were excluded from these actions were those of us who actually worked in the sex industry. Nobody even bothered to ask us what we thought."

In the same year Kathleen Barry, author of *Female Sexual Slavery*, organised a conference on that subject in Rotterdam. Dolores French, who flew to Holland to attend, explains how she and fellow activist Margo St. James were excluded from the proceedings, as the organiser, "felt that prostitutes were too brainwashed and oppressed to represent themselves, that we were all slaves to our pimps".

French and St. James have been two of the key figures in the politicisation of prostitutes in the United States. It was Margo St. James who in 1973 founded the first pressure-group to campaign for prostitutes. COYOTE, Call Off Your Old Tired Ethics, published an influential newsletter, *Coyote Howls*, and generally made its voice heard, financing itself through an annual "Hookers' Ball". From this grew the National Task Force on Prostitution, formed by St. James and the lesbian feminist Priscilla Alexander. In addition a host of flamboyant acronyms joined COYOTE. In New York, prostitutes formed PONY; in Massachusetts, PUMA; in Kansas City, KITTY; in

CHARLIE ARCHAMBAULT: *Dolores French, c. 1988*

San Diego, OCELOT; and so on. Dolores French founded HIRE (Hooking Is Real Employment) in Atlanta, Georgia, and was appointed to the Mayor's Task Force on Prostitution (1985-6).

Elsewhere in the world, the ferment of ideas and arguments stirred up by the Women's Liberation movement was likewise reflected in a growth of self-confidence and outspokenness among prostitutes. Famously, prostitutes in Lyons, France, soon organised into the French Collective of Prostitutes, staged a strike in 1975, and occupied a church in protest at police harassment and the failure of police to pursue a serial killer who was attacking prostitutes. The massive press attention on this "Hookers' strike" focused people's minds as never before on the rights and wrongs of prostitution, and the rights and wrongs of prostitutes.

In England, Helen Buckingham took the opportunity offered by the publication in 1975 of Jeremy Sandford's sympathetic collection of interviews, *Prostitutes*, to launch PUSSI, Prostitutes United for Social and Sexual Integration, which later became, rather more tamely, PLAN, Prostitution Laws Are Nonsense. An English Collective of Prostitutes was formed within the Wages for Housework Campaign.

Similar organisations sprung up all over the world: West Germany, Italy, Switzerland, Canada, Australia, the Netherlands. Alliances among women in all these countries led to an International Committee for Prostitutes' Rights, co-directors Margo St. James and Gail Pheterson. The First World Whores' Congress was held in Amsterdam in 1985; the Second at the European Parliament in Brussels in 1986.

Not all those who spoke out agreed with COYOTE's liberal view of women's right to choose prostitution; the English Collective of Prostitutes, for instance, argues that prostitution is always a matter of economic necessity, while the ex-prostitutes who formed WHISPER (Women Hurt in Systems of Prostitution Engaged in Revolt) argue that all prostitution is part of a system of male oppression. All of these views, from the prostitute as victim to the prostitute as free agent, or independent businesswomen, had perhaps been heard before, but never from the prostitutes themselves, and it was the compelling authenticity of what they had to say which caught the attention of all who heard them. One contributor to the excellent anthology *Sex Work: Writings by Women in the Sex Industry*, Carol Leigh, known as "Scarlot Harlot", caught some of the heady mood of the times: "Ah, when whores start telling the truth, and lifting the burden of these lies we will become so powerful and the future of prostitution will be so rosy . . . "

In general, the demands of prostitutes can be summed up as decriminalisation of prostitution entered into by individual adult choice, together with strong enforcement of laws against "fraud, coercion, violence, child sexual abuse, child labor, rape and racism". The "World Charter for Prostitutes' Rights" hammered out in Amsterdam in 1985, from which this quotation comes, argues eloquently for a radical reform of laws and attitudes.

EDWARD BURRA: *Ladies Walking, c. 1947*

Prostitution should be treated like any other business, paying taxes and receiving benefits in the normal way. Prostitutes should be guaranteed "all human rights and civil liberties, including the freedom of speech, travel, immigration, work, marriage and motherhood and the right to unemployment insurance, health insurance and housing." That any group in our society should have to *argue* for such basic rights as this tells its own story of oppression.

As with most such campaigns, progress seems to have been one step forwards and two steps back, and prostitutes' rights, far from being more respected, have been further eroded by the scapegoating of prostitutes for the spread of heterosexual AIDS. For most politicians, prostitution is still a "social evil" to be eradicated, and any improvement of working conditions for prostitutes can be construed as condoning prostitution. There are very few votes in supporting prostitutes.

Where political change does occur, it tends to cater to the customer's satisfaction – most politicians being men – rather than the worker's. An example is the West German Eros Centres. Allan Mankoff's consumer guide to *Lusty Europe* had no reservations about recommending these to readers. He wrote of the Hamburg Eros Centre, "This is the ultimate cathouse of the computer age." Prostitute F., interviewed by Claude Jaget, had a different perspective: "It's worse than science fiction, a society completely organised around the men who've got enough cash, for their pleasure."

Another example might be the use of sexual services to boost tourism, as has happened most notably in Thailand. A local tradition of prostitution, distorted by "rest-and-recreation" trips for GIs in Vietnam, has produced in Thailand a sort of prostitution of an entire culture. The charm and helpfulness of the Thai character are themselves "sold" to every tourist, so that the difference between natural and assumed charm loses its meaning. Package tours from Japan and Germany are frankly based on readily available cheap sex, of the kind that was celebrated in Justin Wintle's 1977 novel, *Paradise for Hire*, which, he notes in his more sober post-AIDS travelogue *Heat Treatment*, was "little more than a transposed diary I kept of my first visit to Thailand in 1977". In his experience, "the majority of waitresses, if given the smallest encouragement, were as available as the official hookers. And the same went for many bank clerks and shop assistants." One 1986 estimate gave a figure of 700,000 female prostitutes out of a Thai population of 55 million.

The blatant exploitation of the poor by the rich that one finds in Thailand or the Philippines is reminiscent of nineteenth-century Europe: in London,

ANONYMOUS PHOTOGRAPH: *Ulla, leader of the French hookers' strike, 1975*

for instance, guided tours of the "low lodging-houses" in which street prostitutes lived were a popular tourist attraction. So has nothing changed? Not much. But things may be on the move. In March 1991 Mechai Viravaidya, the Minister of the Prime Minister's office in Thailand's new military government, announced to the world: "Sex tourists are no longer welcome here. We are telling them to go back home and exploit their own women and children."

Prostitutes have found a voice, even if that voice is still often muffled by

R.B. KITAJ: *Frankfurt Brothel, 1978*

BERT HARDY: *A girl in her room, Barcelona, 1951*

society's disapproval. No one could forget the sight of Dolores French being interviewed on a prime-time British talk show by a female broadcaster who, faced with one of the most intelligent and articulate spokeswomen for prostitutes' rights, could only splutter, "Do you feel no shame?" Prostitutes still have some way to go before women in general take up their cause with the vigour and effect with which Josephine Butler campaigned for them in the last century. The author Gay Talese could get credit for innovation and imagination when he owned up to having spent several months running a massage parlor in New York as research for his book on the sexual revolution, *Thy Neighbour's Wife*, but if he had been a woman, and instead of managing a massage parlor had worked in one, the authority of his argument would have been undermined rather than strengthened for many readers.

Talese's book describes the free sexuality at John and Barbara Williamson's Sandstone community in California, championed by Dr Alex Comfort in his *More Joy of Sex*, tracing the community's roots in the American Utopian tradition best exemplified by John Humphrey Noyes's Oneida settlement in New York State, a nineteenth-century experiment in eugenics and "complex marriage". He also notes how such ventures were commercialised in cities such as New York, where "Plato's Retreat" opened to provide a luxurious setting for single, multiple and group sexual encounters, a sexual free-for-all in which everyone was both prostitute and customer at once. At the height of its – pre-AIDS – popularity, a thousand couples a week joined the never-ending orgy at Plato's. It was the apotheosis of the sexual revolution, and did, in its way, suggest a new form of prostitution among equals, by-passing the traditional power-plays and moral resentments.

Plato's Retreat and its imitators were a distinctly American variation on the classic French *partouze*. The *partouze* is essentially a private partner-swapping party. One of Allan Mankoff's informants told him, "Of course the private *partouzes* are the best of all – among friends and carefully selected guests. It is very difficult to succeed in *partouzes*. Everyone must be beautiful, clever, and sensitive, or at least two of the three." The growth of "swinger" clubs in the USA was mirrored by the opening of public *partouze* houses in France, which were not illegal because customers were not paying for sex; they were for couples only, though some men were known to bring prostitute partners. In some ways, again, these houses redefined prostitution for a new age, while harking back in many essentials to the grand brothels of the past. Mankoff describes, for instance, the luxurious fittings of a *partouze* house in the rue Le Chatelier, admiring,

> the *fin-de-siècle* garnishings – some lovely rural prints and tasteful nudes, all handsomely framed; delightful glass-encased doll collection in the

BERYL COOK: *Bed Show, 1988*

sumptuous, highly polished ground-floor parlor . . . And the service is fantastic. Three uniformed maids are in constant attendance on the twenty to forty gamboling couples who may visit Le Chatelier in the course of an evening.

The question remains how much male/female relationships can develop within their present frameworks of "ownership" (in marriage) and "buying" (in prostitution). The very act of sexual intercourse has been interpreted by some feminist thinkers as a parable of male domination, with the invasion of the woman by the man. One can but grasp at straws in the wind: the 1991 decision by the English Lord Chief Justice that husbands can, after all, be found guilty of raping their wives; the terminology of the prostitutes' clients who told Eileen McLeod that what they most enjoyed with prostitutes was "a nice playaround".

One might hope that society would some day reach the point where prostitution disappeared, both because women no longer saw selling sex as their only hope of making money, and because men no longer wanted to buy sexual favours. In the run-up to this unlikely future, it seems ridiculous to continue to criminalise, marginalise and isolate prostitutes, and to confuse forced and voluntary prostitution. The paraphernalia of repression currently used against prostitutes actually encourages abuse and exploitation, and is manifestly incapable of suppressing prostitution. Perhaps its best to leave the last word to a prostitute, E., who told Claude Jaget:

> The world of prostitution is like a drug. Even a girl who stops always comes back to this world; not as a prostitute, but she keeps up her contacts, her friends. When you know it, it's extremely lively, it's exciting, it's a fascinating world. There's a kind of freedom you don't find anywhere else.

NOTES

No life is long enough to read, let alone evaluate, the literature of prostitution. In the Bibliography I have listed the works which were most useful to me in writing the present book, but it seems worthwhile also to list here, chapter by chapter, the source and background material which will be most immediately helpful to those seeking to pursue any point in the text. Anyone who troubles to do so will see the great debt I owe to the researches of others, and I would like here to record my gratitude to all the writers listed in the Bibliography, and especially to those whose work I have quoted. Having rejected the notion of footnotes as inappropriate for a work of this nature, I have tried nevertheless to make clear the source of all quotations, either in the main text or in the notes, in order to direct other researchers to the primary material. A word of caution is perhaps necessary in the evaluation of the autobiographies of prostitutes and madams. While many of these are genuine, and some of them have provided this book with its most vivid and authentic material, a good many are faked or fictionalised, and some which are cited by other writers on this subject strike me as being distinctly dubious. I have tried to rely only on material whose authenticity is beyond question, but apologise to readers if I, too, have been taken in by a clever fake.

Chapter One

Sex Work: Writings by Women in the Sex Industry edited by Frédérique Delacoste & Priscilla Alexander contains an excellent annotated bibliography which documents the range of feminist reactions to prostitution: the book itself is a particularly valuable contribution to the debate. Gail Pheterson ed., *A Vindication of the Rights of Whores* explores the turbulent issues raised at the first two World Whores' Congresses, held in 1985 and 1986. Laurie Bell ed., *Good Girls/Bad Girls* documents a very lively conference on prostitution and sexual politics held in Toronto in 1985. *A Herstory of Prostitution in Western Europe* by Jess Wells offers a polemical footnote to more conventional studies, among which I would recommend L.F. Henriques' 3-volume *Prostitution and Society*. On a more popular level, *The Oldest Profession* by Hilary Evans is readable and well-researched.

Chapter Two

G.R. Quaife's *Wanton Wenches and Wayward Wives* is an excellent study of "peasants and illicit sex in early seventeenth-century England", based on a close study of contemporary court records. Eighteenth-century prostitution in Britain is vividly portrayed in John Cleland's novel *Memoirs of a Woman of Pleasure* (*Fanny Hill*), and the factual background to this has been investigated with cheerful diligence by E.J. Burford in various books. The nineteenth-century picture has been well surveyed by Ronald Pearsall in *The Worm in the Bud*, while Frances Finnegan's *Poverty and Prostitution: A Study of Prostitutes in York* is an exceptionally detailed account of prostitution in one provincial city. Sexual life in Britain in the twentieth century has been well treated in Stephen Humphries, *A Secret World of Sex*, and Eileen McLeod, *Working Women: Prostitution Now* offers a vivid and excellently organized picture of contemporary prostitution in Birmingham.

Chapter Three

The sexual history of the United States has been thoroughly explored by John D'Emilio & Estelle B. Freedman in *Intimate Matters: A History of Sexuality in America*. Nineteenth-century prostitution is well covered in Anne M. Butler, *Daughters of Joy, Sisters of Misery*. George J. Kneeland's *Prostitution in New York City*, commissioned by the Bureau of Social Hygiene under the chairmanship of John D. Rockefeller Jr., remains an indispensible source, one of many utilised in Ruth Rosen's splendid *The Lost Sisterhood: Prostitution in America, 1900-1918*. Of all the studies of America's red-light districts, Al Rose's *Storyville* stands out, particularly for its fascinating interview material. Charles Winick & Paul M. Kinsie, *The Lively Commerce* is an essential guide to prostitution in twentieth-century America; Kinsie was a former associate of Kneeland. The "sexual revolution" is interestingly covered in Gay Talese *Thy Neighbour's Wife*. Bernard Cohen's *Deviant Street Networks* is an in-depth sociological study of Manhattan street prostitution in the 1970s; *Mayflower Madam* by Sidney Biddle Barrows with William Novak looks at the other side of the coin, in its inside account of a high-class call-girl operation.

Chapter Four

Medieval Prostitution by Jacques Rossiaud and *Prostitution in Medieval Society* by Leah Lydia Otis provide excellent coverage of a fascinating period. Nineteenth-century French prostitution was first studied by Parent-Duchatelet, and his *De la Prostitution dans la Ville de Paris* was the starting point for Jill Harsin's study *Policing Prostitution in Nineteenth-Century Paris*. Zola's novel *Nana* is a brilliant depiction of prostitution in the Second Empire. Allan Mankoff's *Lusty Europe* presents a detailed and fascinating client's-eye overview of prostitution in modern Europe, while *Prostitutes: Our Life* edited by Claude Jaget allows six French prostitutes to state their own case in the aftermath of the French National Hookers' Strike.

Chapter Five

The classic madam's autobiography is Polly Adler's *A House is not a Home*. The business organisation of brothels is examined in Barbara Sherman Heyl, *The Madam as Entrepreneur*. Harold Greenwald has tracked the rise of *The Call Girl*, and the modern workings of the call-girl system have been well explained by Sidney Biddle Barrows in *Mayflower Madam*. Working on the streets is scrutinised by Bernard Cohen in *Deviant Street Networks* and well portrayed in John Davidson, *The Stroll*. The nature of pimping is outlined in *The Second Oldest Profession* by Ben. L. Reitman, and further examined in Christina & Richard Milner, *Black Players*.

Chapter Six

Judith R. Walkowitz, *Prostitution and Victorian Society* examines the controversy surrounding the Contagious Diseases Acts. Barbara Meil Hobson, *Uneasy Virtue: The Politics of Prostitution and the American Reform Tradition* is very well documented, as is Linda Mahood's study of *The Magdalenes*. Abraham A. Sion, *Prostitution and Law* and P.J. Goldstein, *Prostitution and Drugs* are both authoritative in their fields. Mimi H. Sibert, *Sexual Assault of Prostitutes* is a thorough piece of research among 200 San Francisco street prostitutes.

Chapter Seven

Prostitutes' clients are an unusual and welcome focus of attention in Eileen McLeod's *Working Women: Prostitution Now*. Walter's *My Secret Life* remains the most detailed document we have of a client's obsessional pursuit of prostitutes; its eleven volumes have been manageably abridged into one by G. Legman. Martin O'Brien's highly unusual travel book *All the Girls* is a well-written if unthinking account of his encounters with prostitutes across the world, rivalling Walter's claim to have slept with women from "twenty-seven different empires, kingdoms or countries, and eighty or more different nationalities, including every one in Europe except a Laplander."

Chapter Eight

In addition to the books mentioned in the note to the introduction, mention must be made of two important works by Kate Millett: *Sexual Politics* and *The Prostitution*

Papers. A great deal of subsequent writing on these topics derives from these two books. An interesting sidelight on an earlier era, valuable for its relevance to the autobiographies of eighteenth-century prostitutes, is Alice Browne, *The Eighteenth-Century Feminist Mind*. Kathleen Barry's *Female Sexual Slavery* considers the White Slave trade and forced prostitution, while teenage and child prostitution are well covered in D. Kelly Weisberg, *Children of the Night* and Gitta Sereny, *The Invisible Children*.

Chapter Nine

Sexual tourism in Thailand is explored in P. Phongpaichit's U.N. report *From Peasant Girls to Bangkok Masseuses*. Sex workers speak out in Nickie Roberts, *TheFront Line* and Delacoste and Alexander, *Sex Work*, which also contains details of various prostitutes' organisations. Jeremy Sandford, *Prostitutes* and Roberta Perkins & Garry Bennett, *Being a Prostitute* are particularly useful collections of interviews with prostitutes (the latter containing a good deal of material on male prostitution), while of recent prostitutes' autobiographies, *Working: My Life as a Prostitute* by Dolores French with Linda Lee stands out for its frankness, wit and humanity.

BIBLIOGRAPHY

ACTON, WILLIAM *Prostitution Considered in its Moral, Social, & Sanitary Aspects* London: John Churchill 1857

ADLER, POLLY *A House is not a Home* New York: Rhinehart Books 1953

ALEXANDER, PRISCILLA See DELACOSTE

ANON. *Ranger's Impartial List of the Ladies of Pleasure of Edinburgh* Edinburgh: Paul Harris 1978; 1st edn 1775

    Harris's List of Covent-Garden Ladies; or, Man of Pleasure's Kalender for the Year 1788 London: H. Ranger 1788

ASBURY, HERBERT *The Barbary Coast* London: Jarrolds 1934

    The French Quarter London: Jarrolds 1937

BARROWS, SYDNEY BIDDLE, with NOVAK, WILLIAM *Mayflower Madam* London: Macdonald 1986

BARRY, KATHLEEN *Female Sexual Slavery* Englewood Cliffs, N.J.: Prentice-Hall 1979

BASSERMANN, LUJO *The Oldest Profession: A History of Prostitution* New York: Dorset Press 1988

BAUDELAIRE, CHARLES *Intimate Journals* tr. Christopher Isherwood, London: Panther 1969

BELL, LAURIE ed. *Good Girls/Bad Girls: Feminist and Sex Trade Workers Face to Face* Seattle: The Seal Press 1987

BELLOCQ. E.J. *Storyville Portraits* New York: The Museum of Modern Art 1970

BENJAMIN, HARRY & MASTERS, R.F.L. *Prostitution and Morality* London: Souvenir Press 1965

BENNETT, GARRY See PERKINS

BINDER, POLLY *The Truth About Cora Pearl* London: Weidenfeld & Nicolson 1986

BINNY, JOHN See MAYHEW

BLOCH, IWAN *Sexual Life in England Past and Present* London: Francis Aldor 1938

BOSWELL, JAMES *Boswell's London Journal* ed. Frederick A. Pottle Harmondsworth: Penguin 1966

BROWN, PERCY *Round the Corner* London: Faber & Faber 1934

BROWNE, ALICE *The Eighteenth-Century Feminist Mind* Brighton: Harvester 1987

BROWNMILLER, SUSAN *Against Our Will: Men, Women and Rape* Harmondsworth: Penguin 1976

BULLOUGH, VERN *et. al.,* ed. *A Bibliography of Prostitution* New York: Garland Publishing 1977

BURFORD, E.J. *London: The Synfulle Citie* London: Robert Hale 1990

    Royal St James's London: Robert Hale 1988

    Wits, Wenchers and Wantons London: Robert Hale 1986

BUTLER, ANNE M. *Daughters of Joy, Sisters of Misery: Prostitutes in the American West 1865-90* Urbana & Chicago: University of Illinois Press 1985

CAMPBELL, CLARE "Prostitutes Interview Their Clients" in *Marie Claire* (London) No. 27 November 1990

CAMPBELL-KEMP, BRIAN *The Therapist: Memoirs of a Modern Whore* London: Bachman & Turner 1975

CARTER, ANGELA *The Sadeian Woman* London: Virago 1979

CHRISTIANE F. *H: Autobiography of a Child Prostitute and Heroin Addict* London: Arlington Books 1980

COGHLAN, MARGARET *Memoirs of Mrs Coghlan* London: Printed for the Author 1794

COHEN, BERNARD *Deviant Street Networks* Lexington: Lexington Books 1980

CORDELIER, JEANNE & LAROCHE, MARTINE *The Life* London: Secker & Warburg 1978

COUSINS, SHEILA *To Beg I Am Ashamed* London: George Routledge & Sons 1938

CROWLEY, ALEISTER *The Magical Record of the Beast 666: The Diaries of Aleister Crowley* ed. John Symonds & Kenneth Grant, London: Duckworth 1972

DAVIDSON, JOHN as told to LAIRD STEVENS *The Stroll: Inner-City Subcultures* Toronto: NC Press 1986

DAVIS, MILES, with QUINCY TROUPE *Miles: The Autobiography* London: Picador 1990

D'EMILIO, J. & FREEDMAN, ESTELLE B. *Intimate Matters: A History of Sexuality in America* New York: Harper & Row 1988

DELACOSTE, FRÉDÉRIQUE & ALEXANDER, PRISCILLA ed. *Sex Work: Writings by Women in the Sex Industry* London: Virago 1988

DES BARRES, PAMELA *I'm with the Band: Confessions of a Groupie* London: New English Library 1989

DICKENS, CHARLES *Oliver Twist* Harmondsworth: Penguin 1966; 1st edn 1837-9

    A December Vision: His Social Journalism ed. Neil Philip & Victor Neuburg, London: Collins 1986

    Letters from Charles Dickens to Angela Burdett-Coutts 1841-1865 ed. Edgar Johnson, London: Jonathan Cape 1953

DOVER, K.J. *Greek Homosexuality* London: Duckworth 1978

DUNTON, JOHN *The Night-Walker: or, Evening Rambles in Search after Lewd Women* New York: Garland Publishing 1985; 1st edn 1696

EVANS, HILARY *The Oldest Profession: An Illustrated History of Prostitution* Newton Abbot: David & Charles 1979

FAUST, BEATRICE *Women, Sex & Pornography* Harmondsworth: Penguin 1981

FIAUX, LOUIS *Les Maisons de Tolerance: Leur Fermeture* Paris: George Carre 1896

FINNEGAN, FRANCES *Poverty and Prostitution: A Study of Victorian Prostitutes in York* Cambridge: Cambridge University Press 1979

FLEXNER, ABRAHAM *Prostitution in Europe* London: Grant Richards 1914

FORD, SELWYN *The Casting Couch* London: Grafton 1990

FORSTER, MARGARET *Significant Sisters: The Grassroots of Active Feminism 1839-1939* London: Martin Secker & Warburg 1984

FREEDMAN, ESTELLE B. See D'EMILIO

FRENCH, DOLORES, with LEE, LINDA *Working: My Life as a Prostitute* London: Victor Gollancz 1989

GLADSTONE, W.E. *Diaries* ed. M.R.D. Foot & H.C.G. Matthew, Oxford: Oxford University Press 1968–89

GOLDMAN, EMMA *Anarchism and other Essays* 3rd edn. New York: Mother Earth Publishing Association 1917

GOLDSTEIN, PAUL *Prostitution and Drugs* Lexington: Lexington Books 1979

GRAVES, ROBERT *Goodbye to All That* Harmondsworth: Penguin 1960

GRAY, JAMES H. *Red Lights on the Prairies* Toronto: Macmillan of Canada 1971

GREENWALD, DR HAROLD *The Call Girl; A Social and Psychoanalytic Study* London: Elek Books, 1958

HALL, SUSAN & ADELMAN, BOB *Gentleman of Leisure: A Year in the life of a Pimp* New York: New American Library 1972

HARRISON, FRASER *The Dark Angel: Aspects of Victorian Sexuality* London: Fontana 1979

HARRISON, PAUL *Inside the Inner City* Harmondsworth: Penguin 1985

HARSIN, JILL *Policing Prostitution in Nineteenth-Century Paris* Princeton, N.J.: Princeton University Press 1985

HEMYING, BRACEBRIDGE See MAYHEW

HENRIQUES, FERNANDO *Prostitution and Society* London: MacGibbon & Kee 1962-8

HERODOTUS *The Histories* tr. Aubrey de Selincourt & A.R. Burn, Harmondsworth: Penguin 1972

HEYL, BARBARA SHERMAN *The Madam as Entepreneur* New Jersey: Transaction Books 1979

HIRSCHFIELD, MAGNUS *The Sexual History of the World War* New York: The Panurge Press 1934

HITE, SHERE *The Hite Report on Male Sexuality* London: Macdonald 1981

HOBSON, BARBARA MEIL *Uneasy Virtue: The Politics of Prostitution and the American Reform Tradition* New York: Basic Books 1987

HOLLIDAY, BILLIE, with DUFTY, WILLIAM *Lady Sings the Blues* London: Sphere 1973

HOLLOWAY, JOHN & BLACK, JOAN ed. *Later English Broadside Ballads* London: Routledge & Kegan Paul 1975-9

HUDSON, DEREK *Munby: Man of Two Worlds* London: Abacus 1974

HUMPHRIES, STEVE *A Secret World of Sex: Forbidden Fruit, The British Experience 1900-1950* London: Sidgwick & Jackson 1988

ICEBERG SLIM *Pimp: The Story of My Life* London: Star 1987

JAGET, CLAUDE ed. *Prostitutes: Our Life* Bristol: Falling Wall Press 1980

KEATING, PETER ed. *Into Unknown England: Selections from the Social Explorers 1866-1913* London: Fontana 1976

KEEFE, LYNN *How Did a Nice Girl Like You Get Into This Business?* London: Sphere 1970

KNEELAND, GEORGE J. *Commercialized Prostitution in New York City* London: Grant Richards 1913

LEVINE, JUNE & MADDEN, LYN *Lyn: A Story of Prostitution* London: The Women's Press 1988

LEVY, NORMA *I, Norma Levy* London: Blond & Briggs 1973

LEWIS, NORMAN *Naples '44* London: Collins 1978

LOMAX, ALAN *Mister Jelly Roll: The Fortunes of Jelly Roll Morton, New Orleans Creole and "Inventor of Jazz"* 2nd edn Berkeley: University of California Press 1973

LOVATT, GLORIA & COCKRILL, PAM *A Nice Girl Like Me* London: Futura 1989

MACKEY, THOMAS C. *Red Lights Out: A Legal History of Prostitution, Disorderly Houses, and Vice Districts 1870-1917* New York: Garland Publishing 1987

MADELEINE *Madeleine: An Autobiography* New York: Persea Books 1986; 1st edn 1919

MAHOOD, LINDA *The Magdalenes: Prostitution in the Nineteenth Century* London: Routledge 1990

MAITLAND, MARIA See PHILLIPS, PHEBE

MALCOLM X, with HALEY, ALEX *The Autobiography of Malcolm X* Harmondsworth: Penguin 1968

MANKOFF, ALLAN H. *Mankoff's Lusty Europe* St Albans: Mayflower 1975

MASS-OBSERVATION *The Pub and the People* London: The Cresset Library 1987; 1st edn 1943

MAUPASSANT, GUY DE "Madame Tellier's Establishment" ("La Maison Tellier") in *Selected Short Stories* tr. Roger Colet, Harmondsworth: Penguin 1971

MAYHEW, HENRY *London Labour and the London Poor* London: Griffin, Bohn, and Company 1861-2

MCLEOD, EILEEN *Working Women: Prostitution Now* London: Croom Helm 1982

MEYRICK, KATE *Secrets of the 43* London: John Long 1933

MILLETT, KATE *The Prostitution Papers* London: Paladin 1975

    Sexual Politics London: Virago 1977

MILNER, CHRISTINA & RICHARD *Black Players: The Secret World of Black Pimps* London: Michael Joseph 1972

MINGUS, CHARLES *Beneath the Underdog* Harmondsworth: Penguin 1975

MUGA, ERASTO ed. *Studies in Prostitution* Nairobi: Kenya Literature Bureau 1980

MUILMAN, T.C. See PHILLIPS, TERESIA CONSTANTIA

MUNBY, A J. See HUDSON

MURPHY, EMMETT *Great Bordellos of the World: An Illustrated History* London: Quartet 1983

MURTAGH, JOHN M. & HARRIS, SARA *Cast the First Stone* New York: McGraw Hill 1957

NORWICH, JOHN JULIUS *Byzantium: The Early Centuries* Harmondsworth: Penguin 1990

O'BRIEN, MARTIN *All the Girls* London: Macmillan 1982

OTIS, LEAH LYDIA *Prostitution in Medieval Society: The History of an Urban Institution in Languedoc* Chicago & London: The University of Chicago Press 1985

PALMER, ROY *The Sound of History: Songs and Social Comment* Oxford: Oxford University Press 1988

PARENT-DUCHATELET, A.J.B. *La Prostitution dans la Ville de Paris* Paris: J.-B. Baillière et Fils 1857

PEARSALL, RONALD *The Worm in the Bud: The World of Victorian Sexuality* London: Weidenfeld & Nicolson 1969

PEPYS, SAMUEL *The Diary of Samuel Pepys* ed. Robert Latham & William Matthews, London: Bell & Hyman 1985

PERKINS, ROBERTA & BENNETT, GARRY *Being a Prostitute: Prostitute Women and Prostitute Men* Sydney: George Allen & Unwin 1985

PHETERSON, GAIL ed. *A Vindication of the Rights of Whores* Seattle: The Seal Press 1989

PHILLIPS, PHEBE *The Woman of the Town: or, Authentic Memoirs of Maria Maitland, well known in the vicinity of Covent Garden* London: J. Roe & Ann Lemoine 1809

PHILLIPS, TERESIA CONSTANTIA *An Apology for the Conduct of Mrs Teresia Constantia Phillips* London: Published by the Author 1748

    A Letter Humbly Address'd to the Right Honourable the Earl of Chesterfield by Mrs Teresia Constantia Muilman London: Printed for the Author 1750

PHONGPAICHIT, P. *From Peasant Girls to Bangkok Masseuses* Geneva: International Labor Office 1982

PINZER, MAIMIE See ROSEN & DAVIDSON

QUAIFE, G.R. *Wanton Wenches and Wayward Wives: Peasants and Illicit Sex in Early Seventeenth Century England* London: Croom Helm 1979

REITMAN, BEN L. *The Second Oldest Profession: A Study of the Prostitute's "Business Manager"* New York: The Vanguard Press 1931

ROBERTS, NICKIE *The Front Line: Women in the Sex Industry Speak* London: Grafton 1986

ROCHESTER, EARL OF See WILMOT

ROSE, AL *Storyville, New Orleans* Alabama: University of Alabama Press 1974

ROSEN, RUTH *The Lost Sisterhood: Prostitution in America 1900-1918* Baltimore & London: The John Hopkins University Press 1982

ROSEN, RUTH & DAVIDSON, SUE, ed. *The Maimie Papers* London: Virago 1979

ROSSIAUD, JACQUES *Medieval Prostitution* tr. Lydia G. Cochrane, Oxford: Basil Blackwell 1988

ROWNTREE. B. SEEBOHM & LAVERS, G.R. *English Life and Leisure: A Social Study* London: Longmans, Green and Co. 1951

SANDFORD, JEREMY *Prostitutes* London: Abacus 1977

SANGER, WILLIAM W. *The History of Prostitution: Its Extent, Causes, and Effects Throughout the World* New York: Harper & Brothers 1859

SCARLET, IAIN *The Professionals: Prostitutes and their Clients* London: Sidgwick & Jackson 1972

SERENY, GITTA *The Invisible Children: Child Prostitution in America, West Germany and Great Britain* London: André Deutsch 1984

SHEEHY, GAIL *Hustling* New York: Delacorte Press 1973

SHELDON ANN *Authentic and Interesting Memoirs of Miss Ann Sheldon* London: Printed for the Authoress 1787-8

SILBERT, MIMI H. *Sexual Assault on Prostitutes: Phase One* Washington D.C.: National Center for the Prevention and Control of Rape, National Institute of Mental Health 1980

SION, ABRAHAM A. *Prostitution and the Law* London: Faber & Faber 1977

SMITH, JOAN *Misogynies* London: Faber & Faber 1989

STEIN, MARTHA L. *Lovers, Friends, Slaves: Nine Male Sexual Types: Their Psycho-Sexual Transactions with Call Girls* New York: Berkeley Pub. Co. & P.T. Putman's Sons 1974

TABOR, PAULINE *Pauline's* Louisville, Ky.: Touchstone 1971

TALESE, GAY *Thy Neighbour's Wife* London: William Collins 1980

TANNAHILL, REAY *Sex in History* London: Cardinal 1989

TAYLOR, ALLEGRA *Prostitution: What's Love Got to Do with It?* London: Optima 1991

TYTLER, JAMES See ANON.

VARGAS, AVA, comp. *La Casa de Cita: Mexican Photographs from the Belle Epoque* London: Quartet 1986

VICINUS, MARTHA ed. *Suffer and Be Still: Women in the Victorian Age* Bloomington: Indiana University Press 1972

VILLON, FRANÇOIS *The Poems of François Villon* tr. Galway Kinnell, New York: Signet 1965

VOGLIOTTI, GABRIEL R. *The Girls of Nevada* Secaucus N.J.: The Citadel Press 1975

WALKOWITZ, JUDITH R. *Prostitution and Victorian Society: Women, Class, and the State* Cambridge: Cambridge University Press 1980

WALTER *My Secret Life* ed. G. Legman, New York: Grove Press 1966

WARD, EDWARD *The London-Spy* New York: Garland Publishing 1985; 4th edn 1709

WEDEKIND, FRANZ *Diary of an Erotic Life* ed. Gerhard Hay, tr. W.E. Yuill, Oxford: Basil Blackwell 1990

WEISBERG, D. KELLY *Children of the Night: A Study of Adolescent Prostitution* Lexington: Lexington Books 1975

WELLS, JESS *A Herstory of Prostitution in Western Europe* Berkeley: Shameless Hussy Press 1982

WILLIAMSON, JOSEPH *Father Joe: The Autobiography of Joseph Williamson of Poplar and Stepney* London: Hodder & Stoughton 1963

WILMOT, JOHN, EARL OF ROCHESTER *The Complete Poems* ed. David M. Vieth, New Haven & London: Yale University Press 1968

WILSON, HARRIETTE *Memoirs of Herself and Others* London: Peter Davies 1929; 1st edn 1825

WINN, DENISE *Prostitutes* London: Hutchinson 1974

WINICK, CHARLES & KINSIE, PAUL M. *The Lively Commerce: Prostitution in the United States* Chicago: Quadrangle Books 1971

WINTLE, JUSTIN *Paradise for Hire* London: Secker & Warburg 1984
Heat Treatment Harmondsworth: Penguin 1990

ZOLA, EMILE *Nana* tr. George Holden, Harmondsworth: Penguin 1972

PICTURE CREDITS

The illustrations are reproduced courtesy of:

7 Musée d'Orsay, Paris/Bridgeman Art Library; *10* Musée Condee, Chantilly/Giraudon/Bridgeman Art Library; *14* Louvre, Paris/Bridgeman Art Library; *15* Musée d'Orsay, Paris, © Réunion des Musées Nationaux; *16* courtesy of Lee Friedlander, New York; *19* Soprintendenza Archeologica di Napoli/British Museum Publications; *23* Historical Portraits Ltd, London/Bridgeman Art Library; *26* Upton House, Oxfordshire/Bridgeman Art Library; *31* Tate Gallery, London; *32* from G.A. Sala *Twice Round the Clock*, 1859; *35* Tate Gallery, London; *39* © Paul Gopal-Chaudhury, courtesy of Benjamin Rhodes Gallery, London; *43* courtesy of Quartet Books Ltd, from *La Casa de Cita* compiled by Ava Vargas, 1986; *44* Hulton Picture Company, London; *47* from the collection of the New Britain Museum of American Art, Connecticut, Harriet Russell Stanley Fund, photo E. Irving Blomstrann; *49* Amon Carter Museum, Fort Worth, Texas, Mazzulla Collection; *51* photograph © 1990 The Art Institute of Chicago, All Rights Reserved, oil on canvas 121.9 × 91.1 cm., Friends of American Art, 1925.295; *55* courtesy of Quartet Books Ltd, from *La Casa de Cita* compiled by Ava Vargas, 1986; *56* courtesy of Lee Friedlander, New York; *59* courtesy of Quartet Books Ltd, from *La Casa de Cita* compiled by Ava Vargas, 1986; *63* Mary Evans Picture Library, London; *67* Musée Carnavalet, Paris/Lauros-Giraudon/Bridgeman Art Library; *69* © 1976 Brassaï, courtesy of Madame Gilberte Brassaï; *70* collection, The Museum of Modern Art, New York, acquired through the Lillie P. Bliss Bequest, oil on canvas 243.9 × 233.7 cm., © DACS 1991; *73* Amon Carter Museum, Fort Worth, Texas, Mazzulla Collection; *75* Thyssen-Bornemisza Collection, Lugano, Switzerland; *79* Mary Evans Picture Library, London; *80* Hulton Picture Company, London; *83* Musée Toulouse-Lautrec, Albi/Bridgeman Art Library; *85* whereabouts unknown; *87* © Otto Dix Stiftung, Vaduz, Liechtenstein; *91* Musée d'Orsay, Paris/Bridgeman Art Library; *95* Christie's, London/Bridgeman Art Library, © DACS 1991; *98* Staatsgalerie, Stuttgart/Bridgeman Art Library, © Otto Dix Stiftung, Vaduz, Liechtenstein; *103* © Otto Dix Stiftung, Vaduz, Liechtenstein; *105* private collection; *107* Musée des Augustins, Toulouse/Giraudon/Bridgeman Art Library; *109* Mary Evans Picture Library, London; *111* Kunsthalle, Hamburg/Bridgeman Art Library; *112* from *Women* compiled by Jim Harter, Dover Books 1982; *114* Musée des Beaux-Arts, Bordeaux/Bridgeman Art Library; *119* Gavin Graham Gallery, London/Bridgeman Art Library; *123* National Gallery, London; *127* photograph © 1990 The Art Institute of Chicago, All Rights Reserved, oil on canvas 80.2 × 60.5 cm., Gift of Mr and Mrs Carter H. Harrison, 1936.11; *130* © R.B. Kitaj, courtesy of Marlborough Fine Art (London) Ltd; *133* courtesy of Dolores French; *135* 135 Victoria & Albert Museum, London/Bridgeman Art Library, © Estate of Edward Burra

administered by Alex Reid & Lefevre Ltd, London; *137* Hulton Picture Company, London; *138* © R.B. Kitaj, courtesy of Marlborough Fine Art Fine Art (London) Ltd; *140* Hulton Picture Company, London; *142* from *Beryl Cook's London* (John Murray, 1988), © Beryl Cook,reproduced by permission of Rogers, Coleridge & White Ltd, original painting exhibited at Portal Gallery Ltd, London. *5, 11, 144, 148, 153, 155* from *1001 Spot Illustrations of the Lively Twenties* compiled by Carol Belanger Grafton, Dover Publications, 1986.

Every effort has been made to trace copyright owners, and the publishers apologize for any inadvertent breach of copyright. The publishers would like to thank all the organisations and individuals listed above for their help. Individuals appearing in the illustrations may be artists' and photographers' models and it is not implied that they are or were engaged in prostitution.

INDEX